Faith & Reflection

Jeffrey Tiel

Copyright © 2013 Jeffrey Tiel

All rights reserved.

ISBN-10: 978-1490392172
ISBN-13: 1490392173

FOR SAINT JUSTIN MARTYR

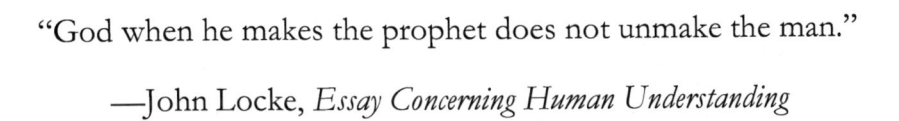

"God when he makes the prophet does not unmake the man."

—John Locke, *Essay Concerning Human Understanding*

ACKNOWLEDGEMENTS

This book is the result of my own participation in and reflection upon the rich philosophical and religious traditions that have influenced us since Socrates and Jesus. I count it an honor to count as collaborators on this project the many students in the classroom with whom I have engaged these questions. I am further deeply appreciative of the many friends and family members who have shared conversations on these topics far too late into too many evenings. For significant editorial assistance and preparation of the final manuscript, I am most grateful to Sarah Black. For the graphic design and original cover artwork, *The Contemplative Virgin*, I am indebted to Joshua Adam Risner.

FOREWORD

When trying to describe what this book is about, the image that comes to my mind is Hopscotch. Strange, I know. But recall the Hopscotch outline on the ground, as your feet moved from one square to two squares back to one and then back to two. Philosophy and religion can be thought of as two separate disciplines but, ultimately, they engage us in one life. In this book, I attempt to recreate this feel, taking a turn into philosophy, but then swerving back to religion, and then pulling them together. You might think of my employing a needle and thread, attempting to weave together a seam that perhaps should never have come apart.

I have divided this book into two parts. Part I focuses on theory, the epistemology (what can we know?) and metaphysics (what is real?) of faith. Are faith and reflection even compatible? Can miracles ever happen? Does God exist? If so, who is he? What is he like? And what about angles, ghosts, and paranormal experiences? Part II turns to the practice of faith, with the narratives of real people engaged with many of the same questions with which we struggle. How do we deal with grief and death? Does faith subtract from the joy of life? Does faith hide from the stark realities of experience? What do the gods really want with us? What is religion *for*?

We will look primarily to the Western philosophical and Christian traditions in order to explore answers to these (and many other) questions. In so far as many of the concepts present in Western Roman thought are also located within the great Eastern Orthodox Christian tradition, much of what is discussed here will be found prescient to the Orthodox. But for Western Christians in particular, there are practical theological considerations within Orthodoxy that exceed the scope of this book. For example, if you ask an Orthodox monk about theology, you might be surprised to receive a suggestion that you pray. Not that you should pray for enlightenment (though that might be part of it too), but rather that the Orthodox don't tend to divide theory and practice the way the West does. Theology is something *done* in the Orthodox tradition, not merely *known*. So, if you wish to really understand Orthodoxy, you would be best served by praying the liturgy of the Church for a whole church year! That's something that might strike Western ears as rather novel, and it's just one of the many fascinating insights available from the other *half* of the Church.

But for our purposes, we will situate ourselves primarily in the West with the occasional dip into Judaism and Paganism. For the Christians viewed themselves as the inheritors of three great traditions: Greco-Roman Philosophy, Jewish Monotheism, and Pagan Religion. St. Justin Martyr pulled these traditions together in his defense of the Faith to the Roman Emperor in his great *Apologia*. C. S. Lewis follows this line of thinking in his compelling novel, *Till We Have Faces*, the book which will provide the finale for our inquiry. In fact, we'll be following in the footsteps of others throughout. For each chapter I'll indicate primary source readings that I encourage you to read too. You might be able to read through Part I without the accompanying readings, but Part II will require that you use this book as a pointer to something truly remarkable, something that you will just have to experience for yourself. Don't miss out.

Table of Contents

Part I

Chapter 1	**Faith & Reflection**	1
	Primary Text: None	
Chapter 2	**Philosophy's Debt to Religion** (Part 1)	7
	Primary Text: Plato, *Apology*	
Chapter 3	**Philosophy's Debt to Religion** (Part 2)	13
	Primary Text: Plato, *Apology*	
Chapter 4	**Reasoning About Faith** (Part 1)	17
	Primary Text: St. Thomas Aquinas, *Summa Contra Gentiles*, Book 1:1-5	
Chapter 5	**Reasoning About Faith** (Part 2)	24
	Primary Text: St. Thomas Aquinas, *Summa Contra Gentiles*, Book 1:6-9	
Chapter 6	**Inoculation Against Cult** (Part 1)	30
	Primary Text: John Locke, *Essay Concerning Human Understanding*, Book IV:18	
Chapter 7	**Inoculation Against Cult** (Part 2)	37
	Primary Text: John Locke, *Essay Concerning Human Understanding*, Book IV:19	

Chapter 8	**Miracles (Part 1)**...	42
	Primary Text: John Locke, *Discourse of Miracles*	
Chapter 9	**Miracles (Part 2)**...	49
	Primary Text: David Hume, "Miracles" (from his *Enquiry Concerning Human Understanding*)	
Chapter 10	**The Cosmological Argument**	53
	Primary Text: David Hume, *Dialogues Concerning Natural Religion*, Part IX	
Chapter 11	**The Divine Nature: Omnipotent Power**...............	63
	Primary Text: C. S. Lewis, *The Problem of Pain*, Chapter 2	
Chapter 12	**The Divine Nature: Goodness**..............................	70
	Primary Text: *Summa Contra Gentiles*, Book I:37-41; C. S. Lewis, *The Problem of Pain*, Chapter 3	
Chapter 13	**The Divine Nature: Love**......................................	78
	Primary Text: C. S. Lewis, *The Problem of Pain*, Chapter 3	
Chapter 14	**The Existence of Angels**......................................	85
	Primary Text: Peter Kreeft, *Angels (and Demons)*	
Chapter 15	**The Nature of Angels**	92
	Primary Text: Peter Kreeft, *Angels (and Demons)*	

Part II

Chapter 16	**The Shining Barrier**	102
	Primary Text: Sheldon Vanauken,	
	A Severe Mercy, Chapters 1-3	
Chapter 17	**Encounter with Light**	110
	Primary Text: Sheldon Vanauken,	
	A Severe Mercy, Chapter 4	
Chapter 18	**God & the Shining Barrier**	117
	Primary Text: Sheldon Vanauken,	
	A Severe Mercy, Chapter 5	
Chapter 19	**The Barrier Breached**	121
	Primary Text: Sheldon Vanauken,	
	A Severe Mercy, Chapter 6	
Chapter 20	**A Severe Mercy**	126
	Primary Text: Sheldon Vanauken,	
	A Severe Mercy, Chapters 7-10	
Chapter 21	**The Problem of Evil**	133
	Primary Text: David Hume, *Dialogues Concerning*	
	Natural Religion, Parts X-XI	
Chapter 22	**Quilted Religion**	140
	Primary Text: Thomas Howard, *Christ the Tiger*,	
	Parts 1-2 (Pages 1-112)	

Chapter 23   **Transfiguration**... 145

                    Primary Text: Thomas Howard, *Christ the Tiger*,

                    Part 3 (Pages 113ff)

Chapter 24   **A Challenge to the Gods**................................... 149

                    Primary Text: C. S. Lewis, *Till We Have Faces*,

                    Pages 1-76

Chapter 25   **The Sisters' Duel**...156

                    Primary Text: C. S. Lewis, *Till We Have Faces*,

                    Pages 77-176

Chapter 26   **Unraveling a Queen** 162

                    Primary Text: C. S. Lewis, *Till We Have Faces*,

                    Pages 177-294

Chapter 27   **The Face of the God**.. 169

                    Primary Text: C. S. Lewis, *Till We Have Faces*,

                    Pages 253-309

Bibliography 175

PART ONE

CHAPTER ONE

FAITH & REFLECTION

Let's start off this plunge into the intersection of reflection and faith by imagining that we are beginning an academic study of geology. Strange, huh? Well, this is philosophy, so what did you expect? If I were a geologist, and if you were all good geology students, then I might start by describing different kinds of rocks, or I might start by telling you about the origin of the earth, or some other way, correct? And you would dutifully write down all these facts, report them on the exam, and believe that they were true.

I wonder if you'd do the same thing in philosophy. Suppose we were working in political philosophy, for example, and suppose further that I offered you a 14-step proof which indicated to you exactly what political party is correct. Would you then change your political views accordingly? No? Ah, maybe that's too controversial an example. Let's offer a less contentious one, perhaps from religion? Suppose I offered you a 23-step proof, indicating the exact nature of the divine and ended this chapter offering you the chance to join the correct religion. Would you join? No?

Hmm . . . very strange. The geologist gets respect, while the philosopher gets ... what? What accounts for the difference between these attitudes? I suppose we might think that geology is a science while religion isn't. But even a cursory look at the history of thought would show that religion and philosophy were sciences long before geology was! That might have your head turning, so perhaps you'd press the point . . . okay, even if religion could be a "science," it certainly isn't a tangible, a concrete science, while geology certainly is concrete (why resist puns anyway?).

Okay, well, let's talk definitions then. A "science" is any theoretical body of knowledge, so philosophy and religion definitely fall into that category. True, religion and philosophy aren't concrete, if by that we mean sensory-based. We can't see God or justice. We can't smell truth or friendship, can we? But does that mean that they are any less real? Can we suppose that things are real only if they are visible? If so, then our atomic theorists might object. So will our mathematicians, who always thought that they were dealing with the realities that underlie the sensory. They might even be tempted to say that what we take to be visible depends upon a foundation that is invisible. The religious person would likely smile at this thought.

So, we haven't gotten very far in distinguishing our reactions to geology and our reactions to philosophy, have we? Okay, maybe the difference is that whereas geology trades in facts, philosophy and religion merely trade in opinions. Thus, we can think whatever we want in philosophy but not in geology.

I wonder if we aren't moving too fast now, for what can be meant here by "opinions"? Aren't opinions *about* something? Consider what that might be. Let's use an example: suppose I have the opinion that the number of sea bass in the oceans is far less than it was ten years ago. My opinion is really a belief, isn't it? And we evaluate beliefs according to how well they correspond with the facts. So, to evaluate my opinion/belief about the comparative number of sea bass, we would have to look at the facts. So, what are opinions *about*? About what is, i.e., facts.

Back to the difference between geologists and philosophers! Don't geologists have opinions? Of course they do. Some geologists believe that Yellowstone will erupt as a super volcano fairly soon, while other don't. They cannot both be right. They also cannot both be wrong. Only the facts of what happens to Yellowstone will show whose opinion was valid. In short, opinions fall into two classes: true opinions and false opinions. Just like beliefs. Why? Because opinions are about reality, about facts, and that is as concrete as you can get.

Now let's return to philosophy. Couldn't a philosopher have true or false opinions too? Couldn't we have true or false opinions/beliefs about God, for example? But you might have heard that beliefs about God are different, that God exists to the person who believes in him, but not to the person who doesn't.

Perhaps you can see the trouble with this view. Try to believe in God with all your might. Does the power of your belief bring him into existence? Now try to disbelieve in God with all your might. Does the power of your disbelief negate his existence? Isn't it much more likely that he either exists or he doesn't? You aren't a god and you can't just bring things in and out of existence with your belief! God's existence isn't up to us. So, it makes no sense to declare that it is "true to me" that there is a God but "true to someone else" that there isn't. Either God exists or he doesn't, and our opinions about the fact are either true or they are false. Why? Because there *is* a fact of the matter.

Now, that last comment might have sounded rather dogmatic, and you might feel uncomfortable about it, rather offended in fact. So, let's consider this carefully. First, the argument, and then, our reaction. As to the argument, either God exists or he doesn't, right? I mean, what else could it be? It can't be both, and it can't be neither, on pain of contradiction. So, it must be the case that God either exists or he doesn't. As to our reaction, it's curious that we find an argument "offensive," don't you think? How can an argument prove an offense to anyone? Where is the harm? If we're uncomfortable with that, doesn't that tell us more about our own weaknesses than about the reality of the situation?

But you might object here that when you're at lunch and someone sits down and begins to tell you why you should believe this or that about God or about abortion or about war, that you tend to get miffed. Even if that person purports to have six reasons for his view, we don't say, "Oh, great! Let me grab my pen so that I can take notes. If you are correct, I'll dispense with a false belief and acquire a true one. You'll have done me a favor. But if your reasons prove weak, then I'll have done you a benefit by relieving you of a false view." We never, *ever* think this way, do we? Instead we get mad at being disturbed, and we don't want to hear views with which we disagree. That's why the Baptists never have a Methodist in to preach, or the Catholics a Buddhist, or the Hindus a Muslim! But unless we hear views with which we disagree, how can we ever discard false beliefs and acquire new, true ones? How, in other words, can we grow intellectually? For that matter, how can we grow spiritually if we cannot ever change our minds?

It turns out that a main culprit behind our failure to think this way is that we Americans sometimes accord ideas the status of persons. We identify ourselves with our ideas. "If you attack my ideas, you have launched an attack on me personally!" Thus, assaults on ideas are equated with assaults on persons, i.e., *offenses*.

But is this really true? John Stuart Mill, an English philosopher, said that we ought to regard our ideas as combatants in an arena. We should take our most prized notions and cast them into the arena so that everyone can take his best shot. If they stand, then we have reason to have confidence in them. If they fall, then we have benefited greatly by being relieved of false notions.

But we don't like what Mill is saying, do we? We treat our ideas like a baby closely held and cuddled in our arms—"Don't you mess with my kid!" And what would Mill have us do? Take that intellectual baby by the legs and bash it and bash it and bash it in order to see whether it's really a live one!

We feel so angry though, when someone does this to us, don't we? You can understand why Socrates aroused such ire from his contemporaries. We almost act like our American doctrine of natural rights applies not just to persons, but to ideas as well. All ideas are created equal and must be treated with respect, life, and liberty just like persons . . . but does that sound right to you? *Are* ideas like persons, to be treated the same? Should a false idea and a true idea be accorded the same respect?

Think about cults in America—like the Branch Davidians, for example, a few years ago out in Waco, Texas. Suppose the cult members had listened to someone who disagreed with David Koresh. It's possible, isn't it, that many of those people and their children might be alive today? Of course, we all agree, when it's about cults.

But why do we call them "cults?" How is being an Episcopalian any different from being a Branch Davidian? Why do we call the one a cult and the other a "religion" or a "denomination"? To be consistent, shouldn't we evaluate both groups to determine whether what they are saying is true? We won't know until we look.

I suppose someone might suggest in rebuttal that since all the religions really agree with one another, all this talk of evaluating their ideas is foolishness. But that view doesn't appear to be shared by the religions themselves. Up on the Dome of the Rock in Jerusalem, e.g., there are large signs that proclaim for all to see that the Christian doctrine of the Trinity is false. Obviously, the Christians disagree with that claim! So, the Muslims and the Christians cannot both be right, can they? They disagree about real things. If God exists, he either is triune or he isn't. It cannot be both, on pain of contradiction. So, perhaps it is useful for us to think more carefully about the things that we believe.

Maybe philosophy can be useful to religion, offering clarity and evaluation. Similarly, maybe religion can be useful to philosophy. We'll read Plato's *Apology* for our next chapter, and we're going to discover the origin of philosophy from the world's first philosopher, Socrates, and would you believe that it was *religion*?

CHAPTER TWO

PHILOSOPHY'S DEBT TO RELIGION, PART 1

(Plato, *Apology*)

We begin our first philosophical text, Plato's *Apology*, with two very reasonable questions. First, where's Plato? It seems like Socrates is the main character. And second, why is Socrates apologizing? He doesn't sound very apologetic! Well, these are excellent questions, so let's begin with the first. Plato was the prize student of Socrates. Though Socrates never wrote down any of his philosophical work, his student recorded and developed many of his old master's dialogues. Thus, the author is Plato, but Socrates is the source and the main character. Secondly, Socrates is not apologizing, but defending himself; he's on trial. The old Greek word *apologia* means "defense." (St. Peter uses the term to say that every Christian ought to be readily able to provide an *apologia*, a defense, of his faith.) So, we are privy here to Socrates' attempt to defend himself against three accusers: Meletus, Anytus, and Lycon.

So, who are these guys? They represent the talking heads of Athens, the intellectual elites, the orators, the poets, the politicians and professional men.

They have joined together to bring Socrates to trial . . . but it might be difficult to see it as a trial, since it differs so much from our own trials. Notice that there is no prosecutor, even though this turns out to be a capital case. In our judicial system we distinguish civil trials, where a plaintiff can bring an accusation against a defendant, from criminal trials, where a prosecutor represents the people and the victim against a defendant. Only in our *criminal* trials can a person wind up in prison or on death row. But in Athens there was no distinction in the systems (this was 2,500 years ago, after all), so Socrates faces a capital trial which feels like a civil trial.

Notice, furthermore, that there is no judge! Socrates appeals to the jury for procedural objections ("Gentlemen of the jury, make him answer the question!"). In our time, of course, we have separated the decision procedure in trials into a formal side (the judge) and a substantive side (the jury). But there's no reason in principle that it couldn't be the same body. What is tough for Socrates is the sheer number and behavior of the jurors. There are 501 of them, and they are as noisy as a mob. Moreover, Socrates asks them to testify to one another. So, this is real jury "by peer," by people who actually know him. There is no supposition that they are neutral to the question put to them. They are noisy and reactionary, so Socrates is concerned whether he will be successful in speaking to them. His style of philosophy is one-on-one dialogue, not great speech-making. His accusers, on the other hand, are some of the best orators in human history.

Now, why do you suppose that there are 501 jurors, as opposed to 500? To break ties? Well, yes, but originally the system had just 500 jurors. To understand why this was, we have to peer into Athenian legend and the dark days when the furies raged among men. During that time, criminal situations were dealt with personally, and as you might imagine, this led to blood feuds that lasted for generations. So, at some point the goddess Athena intervened in the city that bore her name, and she gave the city a great gift: the jury system.

Thus, cases could be settled in an organized fashion. But if there were a tie, the gods would settle the matter. That didn't work out well in practice, so somewhere along the way, a 501st juror slipped in. But remember that the entire judicial system in Athens is a divine gift; that'll become quite important later.

One final point about the form of the trial: Socrates has no lawyer. As an Athenian citizen, he was expected to know the law and to be able to employ it. That is quite different from what we expect, nowadays, when the head of the IRS admits that he cannot even do his own taxes—they're that complex! So, Socrates is intimidated by the force of his accusers' arguments (they've had their say before what we read in the text). Socrates is nervous that he won't have enough time to educate his audience about the truth of his life. He is concerned about the prejudices against him. Did you happen to catch what these were?

Socrates refers to three. First, people believe that he investigates things in the heavens and under the earth. That's a euphemistic way of saying that he does natural science (in a way that renders appeals to the gods unnecessary). Second, that he makes the weaker argument appear to defeat the stronger. And lastly, that he teaches these things to others. Those are some hefty prejudices, for if people really believe the second one, then how can he succeed in his defense, even if what he says is right?

These three prejudices relate directly to the two main charges that Meletus and company are bringing against him, namely that he is corrupting the youth and that he is impious, not believing in the gods of the state. Perhaps you can see the connections between the prejudices and the charges. Socrates certainly can, and so he feels forced to confront the prejudices first.

To the first prejudice, he replies that he never took an interest in the natural sciences, that his main interest has been ethics, the human good. Moreover, he explains, those naturalistic teachings actually belong to Anaxagoras, not to Socrates, and everyone knows that. To the second and third prejudices, he offers the puzzling response that he is not a teacher.

Why would the world's first and greatest philosopher deny that he is a teacher? Well, he insists that he does not take fees like the local professional teachers who promise for a fee to teach one's son how to live as an effective and virtuous Athenian nobleman. But Socrates denies the injection model of education, rejecting the notion that virtue can even be taught. Pouring information into someone's brain doesn't entail that he understands anything. Unless someone makes the argument his own, becomes a self-teacher, i.e., he doesn't really know at all. So, Socrates denies the whole exchange model of education: no fees collected in exchange for knowledge injected. Instead, he views the role of a philosopher as identical to that of a midwife. The pregnant mind does all the labor. All Socrates does is assist the person in giving birth to his thoughts and evaluating whether they are live or stillborn births. Thus, the only true teacher is *you*. Think about that, very carefully.

As a result, Socrates cannot be held responsible for his "students," since he never promised to turn them into anything. They are responsible for their own beliefs as well as their own actions. Therefore, making weaker arguments appear stronger and teaching these things to others are not prejudices that have anything to do with Socrates' own style of argument, dialectic, but rather pertain to the style of rhetoric done by his accusers, the sophists.

So, suppose that you were a juror hearing that the prejudices against Socrates which you've heard all your life about him are all false. Wouldn't you wonder how they all got started? Before Socrates challenges the accusations against him directly, he offers us the story of how it all began.

One day his friend Chaerephon paid a visit to the famous Oracle at Delphi. The oracle told him that no one was wiser than Socrates. Socrates found this puzzling because he was merely a stone-cutter by trade and never thought of himself as particularly wise. He couldn't understand the meaning of the god's message, so he decided to search for wise people and see what this message could really mean. He found many forms of wisdom that exceeded him, according to the various arts practiced by the artisans. Shipbuilders knew their art, just as he knew stone-cutting. So, that couldn't be the meaning of the divine message.

But when he searched for wisdom among the city's elites, he ran into a problem. They didn't seem to know what they were talking about. For example, he asked the general Laches about the essence of courage, yet the general became all tongue-tied and unable to answer. The same thing happened when he asked the politicians about justice, the poets about interpretation, and so on. They all thought they knew things that they didn't know, and, when this was exposed, most got mad. Socrates, on the other hand, knew what he didn't know and didn't pretend that he knew something when he didn't. So, he began to think he understood the god's meaning. The god hadn't said that Socrates was the wisest of all, but rather, that none was wiser than he. Thus, Socrates possessed a wisdom that others could possess, and this wisdom was the intellectual humility not to lay claim to what he didn't know, but to search out each thing according to its nature.

So, how did the trouble begin for Socrates? He made many enemies in these public encounters with the talking heads of Athens. The youth found his cross-examinations of public figures exhilarating. Can you imagine if for the next presidential debate, Socrates was called in to ask the questions? None of us would miss that for the world, would we? So, the power-pushers in Athens became furious with Socrates, for the most part. There were some who realized that they needed to inquire about what things like justice, truth, goodness, beauty, friendship, courage, *et al* really are, and so they humbly became philosophers, seeking and loving wisdom. Over time Socrates realized that philosophy—the love of wisdom—was actually a gift from the god to the city of Athens and that he was doing the city a great good. For what could be of greater benefit to a people than a motive toward the highest and most honest human virtues?

Of course, the orators, poets, and politicians didn't change course; they decided to change Socrates from a living person to a corpse, and thus came this trial. Having dealt with the real origin of the prejudice against him, Socrates offers us the principle by which he lives his life: the unexamined life is not worth living. I want you to reflect thoughtfully on this idea. Would you say that it describes your life? If not, why not? What reasons do we have for not examining our lives? Are those good reasons? Perhaps we aren't all that different from the Athenians—too hurried, too lazy, and too proud to humbly subject ourselves to examination. But without examination how can we reject false views to put on true ones? How can we overcome evil habits and replace them with virtues?

Finally, I'd like you to notice something extraordinary about the origin of philosophy: it comes at the behest of the god. In other words, philosophy is not opposed to religion for Socrates, is it? Rather philosophy begins as a religious quest! Notice all the things that philosophers and religious people have in common. Don't both sets talk about truth, about goodness, about ultimate reality, about beauty? There may be much more cross-over between thought and belief, between inquiry and piety, between reflection and faith than we've ever supposed. On the other hand, perhaps there are some differences. Think back to Socrates' principle that the unexamined life is not worth living. Does that apply to religion? Should we subject our religious views to Socratic dialectical review? Is doubt a good thing in church? Much to mull over until our next chapter when we continue on with Socrates' defense.

CHAPTER THREE

PHILOSOPHY'S DEBT TO RELIGION, PART 2

(Plato, *Apology*)

We left off our last chapter mulling over Socrates' view that the unexamined life is not worth living. Without examination we cannot tell where we are going, whether toward beauty or toward ugliness of soul. Examination seems central to what differentiates us from the animals. We possess rationality, that capacity to know universal truth. And we are endlessly motivated to wonder at the world around us. Examination seems essential to our humanity.

But like the ancient Athenians, we find ourselves reluctant to do this kind of examination. We become complacent and comfortable and invested in and lazy about our own views and actions. But as we cease examining, we likewise cease thinking, and our lives do in fact become more tedious, less interesting, less valued.

Let's get back to Socrates' defense. Meletus is now called to the stand to face Socrates directly. This is the moment we've been waiting for, isn't it? Socrates states that his strategy is to show that Meletus is insincere. How is this relevant to his case? I suppose, on the one hand, it seems pretty obvious that if your accuser isn't sincere, then one shouldn't take seriously the accusation. But there's another deeper reason why Socrates' showing that Meletus is insincere is truly a brilliant strategy. You've probably heard of "Perry Mason moments" in trials? The point where the defense lawyer gets up and shows not only did his client not commit the crime, but the District Attorney did! Wow! Those are the biggest moments in trial law. Socrates is plotting just such a move here, for if Meletus is insincere in his charges, then he is insincere and frivolous about divine matters because the jury system was a gift from the gods. So, who then is really impious? Socrates or Meletus? If Meletus is insincere in his views about the education of the youth, yet he is a talking head in Athens, then who is more likely to be corrupting the youth? Socrates or Meletus? You see Socrates' game plan? Socrates intends to flip the charges against his accusers. Not only is Socrates not guilty of impiety or corruption of the youth, but it is actually his *accusers* who are.

Socrates now begins his cross examination of Meletus forcing him to answer his questions. He gets Meletus to admit that he really thinks that everyone in Athens is good for the youth except for that evil Socrates. But of course, no one believes such nonsense in any other area of life. Is everyone a good shipbuilder or only a few? Is everyone a good plumber or only a few? Then why would we suppose that everyone is good for the young and only one person is bad for them? It seems clear that Meletus has never bothered his head about real education, and, therefore, his charges are insincere.

Socrates next takes up the charge of impiety. He asks Meletus whether the issue is that he believes in gods different from the state or rather that he believes in no gods at all. Meletus insists that Socrates doesn't believe in any gods. Socrates scoffs at this and asks Meletus if he really expects the jurors not to realize that he is directly contradicting himself? Meletus doesn't understand this, so Socrates asks him whether it is possible to believe in human things and not in human beings. Meletus admits that it's not. Socrates asks him next if it's possible to believe in divine activities but not divine beings. Again Meletus admits that it's not. Then, why, Socrates wonders, does Meletus think that Socrates disbelieves in divine beings when his entire life is devoted to a divine activity, namely philosophy?

Socrates does a pretty good job of cracking Meletus, so good, in fact, that when he is nonetheless convicted by the jury, the vote is much closer than Socrates had expected. During the penalty phase of the trial, both sides present what they think would be a fit punishment. Meletus and his friends insist on death, while Socrates suggests free maintenance by the state for life, i.e., a state pension. As you might imagine, this led his friends to enormous consternation, but Socrates was serious (in a way) because philosophy was a great benefit for Athens, so why shouldn't the city support it? Nevertheless, Plato and Critobolus and some of the others offer to cover a 3,000 drachma fine for Socrates, so he suggests that instead.

The jurors decide on the death penalty, and Socrates is sentenced to die by drinking a poison called hemlock (if you'd like to read the moving death scene and hear the great dialogue on the immortality of the soul that precedes it, you can read the *Phaedo* which is contained in the collection of five Platonic dialogues, *The Last Days of Socrates*.) He is concerned for his friends and those jurors who truly followed the law and voted in his favor, so he offers some final words of comfort to them. Let's take a look at those now, because they are profoundly important for our reflections on the links between philosophy and religion.

In the final paragraphs of the *Apology* Socrates considers what death is like. He considers two options. Either it is annihilation or it is the transmission of the soul to another place. If it is annihilation, then it is like a dreamless sleep, and who doesn't like a sleep free from dreams? If it is a transmission from this place to another one where the dead are, then Socrates thinks it would be lovely to go there and converse with all the others who were unjustly sentenced to die by unfair trials, as well as to talk to the great Greek heroes pressing them on the questions he's asked all his life. Thus, he thinks that death is either a dreamless sleep or a dialectical heaven!

Furthermore, he adds something remarkable: he is certain that nothing can harm a good man either in life or in death, for his affairs are not a matter of indifference to the gods. Let's take the first part of that claim. Why would he be telling us that nothing can harm a good man, when he's just been sentenced to death? Well, consider what part of a man most centrally makes him who he is. Would you say it is his body or his soul? If you said soul, then ask yourself whether the mob can harm your soul? They cannot. In fact, the only person who can harm your soul is you—by the injustices you commit. Thus, the good man, the just man, need fear nothing.

Second, Socrates assures us of his confidence that the ways of a good man aren't a matter of indifference to the gods. What does that mean? That the gods care about justice. This was quite a claim for him to be making in 400 B.C. Athens, set as it was against the backdrop of Homeric myths loaded with morally questionable gods. Socrates is telling us something extraordinary: the divine nature is just. And that means that justice wins out in the end.

Immortality and the certainty of a divinely just judgment coming from the world's first philosopher! Maybe reflection and faith aren't so far apart, after all?

CHAPTER FOUR

REASONING ABOUT FAITH, PART 1

(St. Thomas Aquinas, *Summa Contra Gentiles*, Bk. 1:1-5)

We move now to our second text in our journey through faith and reflection, *Summa Contra Gentiles*. What a title! Meaning? Summa: "sum of material," Contra: "against," Gentiles: "Pagans." So, put it all together and we get the sum of the material against the pagans. What is he up to? Take a look at chapter 2, paragraph 2, where he states the thesis of the work: "I have set myself the task of making known, as far as my limited powers will allow, the truth that the Catholic faith professes, and of setting aside the errors that are opposed to it." So, St. Thomas is engaged in a work of setting forth the reasons for the Christian views together with showing why opposing arguments are false.

Now, you might notice that I slipped from "Catholic" to "Christian." St. Thomas is writing during the time of the great Christian unity, when for some 1400 years there was but one church, holy and apostolic and catholic, as the great creeds of the church declare. There were no Protestants, no Orthodox, no Anglicans, no Methodists, no Baptists . . . there was simply The Church. You might recall Jesus' last request offered to his Father in prayer in St. John's gospel, namely that the church would remain one, just as he and his Father were one. For 1,400 years the church maintained that unity. And the word "Catholic" means exactly that—Universality, Unity. The term is first used by one of St. John the Apostle's students, St. Ignatius, Bishop of Antioch. He was taught by one of Jesus' closest friends and understood John's teaching on love, authority, truth, and unity. He captured those ideas with the concept of catholicity, universality.

So, St. Thomas Aquinas is a very useful figure to read, now that we just looked at the father of philosophy, Socrates, for St. Thomas is arguably the greatest Christian thinker of all time. He could narrate three different philosophical treatises at the same time, pausing in mid-sentence as the scribes scribbled to keep up, shifting to the next treatise, and then going back to the other one always remembering just where he was. So, we are in for a real treat here, the best of the best, if you like, well before the problems that erupted in the divisions of the Church.

St. Thomas tells us that he wishes to set aside the errors opposed to the faith, but that there are two difficulties that immediately arise. Take a look at paragraph three of that same chapter. First, nobody really remembers the ancient pagan errors, because the Western world has become thoroughly Christian. Only some Vikings are still pagan, and maybe a few Lithuanians. (Remember, our context is the medieval world!) But it's the second problem that really grabs us: how can you defend the central Christian claims when your opponents (the ancient pagans and those currently like them) don't accept your primary texts as authoritative? Yes, that's a real conundrum, isn't it? If you are a Christian, and you wish to share your faith, what do you do when your opponent rejects the authority of the New Testament? Well, St. Thomas notices that at least in the case of Jews, both Christians and Jews share the Hebrew

Bible, the Old Testament, as a common text, so Christians traditionally have tried to show that Jesus is the Christ by appeal to those texts (you can see this amply demonstrated in the sermons in the Acts of the Apostles, as well as in the Gospel of St. Matthew.) Even better, in the case of heretical Christians, the Old and New Testaments are regarded as authoritative. The problem lies with Muslims and pagans neither of whom is much impressed with either the Hebrew Bible or the New Testament. Nevertheless, St. Thomas points out that whether you are a Jew, a Christian, a Muslim, a pagan, or even an atheist, you are still human, and, thus, our common humanity is that to which any person can appeal. Therefore, St. Thomas offers this *Summa Contra Gentiles* as a work of human reason defending the faith and opposing critics. Yes, he does often cite Christian texts, but never in the place of arguments; he appeals to nothing but what is universally accessible. St. Thomas isn't interested in cheating, in arguing in a circle, so he starts with what is common.

Moving now to chapter 3 we note that St. Thomas talks of a two-fold way of truth. Some truths about God exceed all the ability of human reason, while others are fully within the reach of human reason. In the first category, he offers us the example of the Holy Trinity. In the second category, he offers us examples such that God exists, and that he is one, and the like. Now, what are we to make of this distinction?

Some things about God might be discernible based on our moving from effects to cause. Think about the general form of the cosmological argument for God's existence. All that exists came from somewhere, and when we chart it back in time, we come to the Big Bang. And what caused that? What is the first cause? You can see that this might function as an argument for God's existence. There are many arguments like it. What could you discover about God from this argument? Since the argument tries to get at the cause by looking at the effects, we can draw conclusions about God solely from the effects. We could tell that given the complexity of the universe that God is very smart and very powerful. But could we tell that he is three in person but only one in substance, the doctrine of the Holy Trinity? Hardly.

So perhaps it now becomes clearer what St. Thomas means. Some things about God we can figure out just using our minds and applying them to the world, such as God's existence and nature. But other facts about God we might never had known because they wouldn't have followed merely from God's being our Cause, our Creator. But since God is infinitely huge, it follows that there might be countless features of him about which we know nothing. So, there might be many truths that surpass the reach of reason; we simply don't have evidence about these facts. So, some truths about God are accessible to reason, while others are beyond its grasp.

Now, St. Thomas hasn't yet shown us that there *are* any such truths about God, truths that surpass the reach of human reason; he's shown only that there might be. God might be three in person, or four, or twenty-five . . . we'd only know if he told us. You might object that this would render us subject to charlatans who might purport to represent God's communications to men. And you'd be right. Clearly, we'd have to be very careful in reviewing any such claims. We'll address this crucial issue as we progress through the argument.

Moving into Chapter 4, St. Thomas wishes to explore the notion that some truths that are knowable through human reason might also be revealed by God directly, i.e., that there is a small overlap area in the two-fold mode of truth he referred to earlier. Examples? How about the Ten Commandments. Don't you think that those moral principles are absolutely critical to any civilized people? If people killed, robbed, bore false witness against, stole the wives of, and coveted the possessions of each other, how long would such a "society" last? These commandments are the bedrock of any successful civilization, and are thus, absolutely critical. Now, can we use human reason to show that they are true? Yes, there are many complex arguments in Ethics whereby we could justify such rules. So, why would it be useful for God additionally to give these rules to Moses?

St. Thomas offers three reasons why it is most fitting for God to give these principles both through natural reason and through faith. First, he notices that unless God provided them through faith too, few people would ever have known them. Why? Because not everyone is cut out for philosophy! People have real jobs. Other people are just plain lazy. So, it's a divine gift that God would provide these truths both through reason and through faith. Moreover, learning philosophy only comes at the end of your learning, because it is built up upon all other knowledge, so if we had to wait until then to learn these things as knowledge (not as training in piety from our parents, you understand) we'd be old men! Finally, St. Thomas points out the fragility of human reason. Sometimes we make mistakes, but if we make a mistake on one of these issues, the result could be social catastrophe. Thus, it is a divine mercy that we can hold such truths not only by reason, but also by belief.

Let's turn lastly to chapter 5 where St. Thomas wishes to show that faith itself is fitting for human nature, i.e., not undignified. Consider why someone might be worried about this: we're natural creatures endowed with reason, so whatever we need to know ought to be available to our rational minds. If it's not, it's not for us, not meant for us, not fitting for us. So, this is a good issue for St. Thomas to take up.

First, St. Thomas argues that human beings are dissatisfied with the goods of this life, longing for immortality, for happiness, for freedom from the ills of this world. St. Thomas thinks that these are built-in markers to move us toward eternal things, toward God. So, given that we are naturally drawn toward God, it makes sense that God might wish to reveal more of himself than we might have been able to figure out using only natural reason. Second, God's nature is supposed to be infinite, so that we cannot in principle grasp all that could be known about God. Thus, it is fitting for God to reveal some of those extra things through faith. Third, faith helps curb pride and presumption, the tendency for us to think that we know all that we need to know, the pride in thinking that we are better than those of inferior intellects. If God in his monarchial prerogative decided to enter the world as a small baby, born not into a royal house, but instead into the backwoods country of Judea, then that is his right. But think about what that would mean. God loves us all, not just the mighty, not just the intellectually weighty. Bowing low is part of what it means to respond to a king, so St. Thomas thinks that faith helps curb presumption and pride. Finally, St. Thomas cites Aristotle that the noblest and highest things for human beings to know are divine things, for our natures are rational, and rationality is part of the essence of God. Thus, in keeping with our nature it is fitting for us to know the divine nature, and, thus, it is in keeping with our nature for God himself to offer us a more perfect knowledge about himself via belief.

So, let's review what we've learned. St. Thomas tells us that there might well be truths that surpass reason made known to us by God via faith/belief, and that it would be fitting and useful for us if he were to do this. And lastly, while we've looked at truths that are knowable by reason and others that surpass the knowability of reason, let's not confuse this last category with truths that contradict reason, for no contradiction can ever be true. To say of something that it both is and is not, in the same way at the same time, is to declare a necessary falsehood. If the Holy Trinity were the doctrine that God is both three and one in the same way at the same time, then that would prove contradictory and necessarily false. Obviously, this isn't the case, for the truths that surpass reason aren't contradictory, aren't incoherent. We just don't have evidence that they are true, any more than we possess evidence about what is on the opposite side of Alpha Centauri. So, the claim that there are truths that surpass reason mustn't be understood to insist that there are contradictions that are true. Therefore, the "third category" of "truths that contradict reason" isn't a category at all! Contradictions are contradictions for God just as much as they are for us. The Holy Trinity is the doctrine that God is three in person (one way) yet one in substance (another way); thus, there is no contradiction. Therefore, to say that the doctrine of the Holy Trinity is a truth of faith is not to suggest that there is anything incoherent in the doctrine itself, only that using solely natural evidence available to reason, we'd never have figured it out.

CHAPTER FIVE

REASONING ABOUT FAITH, PART 2

(St. Thomas Aquinas, *Summa Contra Gentiles*, Bk. 1:6-9)

In our last chapter we saw how St. Thomas tried to make room for truths of faith, for those truths that exceed the capacity of reason for their confirmation. He argued that since God is infinite and human minds are finite, it follows that there are truths about God to which the human mind lacks access. But lest it be thought that such truths are, therefore, beyond human nature and, thus, unfitting for human beings, St. Thomas continued to argue that God is deeply relevant to human nature, since God is the good of human nature. As the Christian texts report, all things were made by Him and for him; thus, God is the supreme good, the supreme satisfaction of all created objects. They were made to find their completeness in God. St. Augustine is famous for having said that we all possess a God-sized hole in our souls. Thus, the Christians argue, knowledge about God is deeply relevant to human experience, because we find our happiness in God.

But mightn't we object that, surely, if such things were so vital, that God would just make them available to normal human reasoning? St. Thomas countered that God's revealing these additional truths by means of faith is good for all those lacking the time or constitution for scholarship, as well as good for those used to scholarly life, since it reduces their presumption. Thus, the idea that there are important truths for human beings that God reveals by the mode of faith is not unfitting for human beings. Nor is anything incoherent about it, for when St. Thomas said that such truths *surpass* human reason, he never meant that they *contradict* human reason. We'll see more about that in this chapter.

All right, so St. Thomas has done a fairly good job of showing that there might well be truths about God that he might like to reveal to us. But how would he do that? And how would we avoid falling for charlatans? St. Thomas takes up this problem in chapter 6 of the *Summa Contra Gentiles*. He begins by pointing out the lines from the New Testament which emphasize the non-deceptive nature of the Christian apologetic (i.e., defense). The Christians use arguments. That's the first fascinating thing, don't you think? The truths of faith are grounded in argument, even though human reasoning cannot argue directly to them. We'll have to mull over carefully how that will be possible. But the other issue that these texts show is the difference between the Christian accounts, on the one hand, and the fables and myths of the ancients, on the other. The Christians are claiming something quite different from pagan religious experience, something that the writer of the Epistle to the Hebrews regards as the "substance of things hoped for, the evidence of things unseen," i.e., faith (Hebrews 11:1). That's faith, according to the New Testament, and notice that it is evidential and substantial—nothing incompatible with reason. It seems even to make use of reason. How?

In the next paragraphs, St. Thomas explains the Christian argument for the veracity of the truths of faith. He points out the miracles that accompanied the Christian message from Jesus, raising the dead, healings, and the like. He notes the virtue accompanying the Christian people, and he contrasts that to other religions. Moreover, he notes the sincerity and integrity in the deaths of the martyrs who were eyewitnesses to the events they reported. Further, he emphasizes that Christianity doesn't cheat by using the sword to spread its message, nor does it cater to the carnal pleasures by offering people lots of virgins in heaven if they believe. And again, he refers us to the strange character of the original apostles, a bunch of fishermen from the backwoods, hill-country of the Roman Empire. Yet it was these men who turned the world upside down and ultimately brought down the Empire through a wholesale ideological conversion! How, St. Thomas asks, is that to be explained? His answer? These supernatural effects are the result of a supernatural cause, namely God.

So, let's assume that all these things are legitimate, just as St. Thomas reports. How do they function to make the truths of faith, e.g., that God is triune in person though one in substance, plausible? Do you see the trinity in any of the events I referred to in the last paragraph? I don't either. So, what is the connection between these supernatural events and the claim that God is triune?

Well, St. Thomas already explained that no evidence available to reason can confirm the truth of the trinity, so we shouldn't expect that doctrine to be located in those events. Think rather about what those events themselves are supposed to legitimate . . . namely the veracity of Jesus. In other words, these are the reasons to think that Jesus wasn't just some hillbilly rabbi, but was, in fact, just who he said he was, the Son of God. Now, suppose you were persuaded that yes, these things make it very reasonable to believe that Jesus is the Son of God. Then wouldn't you also tend to think that what he says is true? I mean, is God a deceiver? Of course not, you'll reply. Then if God tells you something, it's reliable, isn't it? Even if what he tells you isn't directly confirmable by reason? Yes, IF God really is telling us. Exactly. And that is why St. Thomas (and the ancient defenders of the Christian faith) points to all of these supernatural events—these miracles and signs—in order to show that God is telling us these things, because Jesus is none other than God.

So, to sum the matter up, St. Thomas is arguing that while we cannot directly verify truths of faith, we can indirectly verify them by directly verifying that the messenger who wishes us to believe that these things are from God is, in fact, a messenger from God. We can see the miracles, and that justifies our believing that this man is from God. So, notice how reason plays a critical role in St. Thomas' understanding of faith. Without reason's evaluating whether or not this person really is from God (by examining those signs), we'd never be able to justify belief in the messenger. Thus, faith proceeds through reason. They are not opposed at all.

But what about rival revelations, we might object! Didn't Mohammed also claim to come from God? And don't his followers claim it to be a divine revelation that there is no trinity at all? So, what are we to make of these rival claims? Well, St. Thomas takes that up in the conclusion of chapter 6 and then on into chapter 7 of the *Summa Contra Gentiles*. Specifically, in chapter 6, he addresses Islam and argues that we find a real evidence gap there. Mohammed didn't perform signs or miracles. He wasn't indicated by the previous prophets. He didn't change the world by supernatural means, but by military means. And he appealed to the carnal vices of human nature (a heaven of virginal sex, as well as the permissibility of multiple wives). What is supernatural about any of this, he asks?

Now, I know we're not supposed to evaluate other religions and say negative things about them . . . or are we? Strange that we think that religious matters are some of the most important in life and then we turn around and say that we shouldn't think critically about them! Why do we do that? Does the Constitution protect religious speech in order to cut off religious speech? Hardly. The point is to enable us to argue about it, instead of killing each other over it. St. Thomas thought it well worth arguing about. So has the Church historically. In fact the Christians are famed for trying to persuade the ancient pagan Romans of the truth of the faith by appealing to arguments, not the sword. The Christians were not insurrectionists. So, if we merely accept the claim that no one should think about religion, we've just cut off a great deal of the way in which our religious forefathers thought about the matter. And to be honest with the past, we cannot do that. We have to face it straight up. Christianity and Islam cannot both be true, because they contradict one another. So, what is someone supposed to do with that reality?

Well, St. Thomas is offering us a means to adjudicate the conflict, by appealing to reason. Real faith welcomes the critical eye of reason, because only by reason can faith be verified. And when you compare the facts between Christianity and Islam, St. Thomas is confident that Islam comes up the loser. As you are reviewing the question, ask yourself if you've ever evaluated your faith. Why do you accept it? Does it have a reasoned basis?

The Christians believe that grace does not contradict nature. What God does in adding to human knowledge through faith does not negate what he already has provided to reason. St. Thomas takes up this issue in chapter 7. God is not the author of contradictory truths. He is one God, so what he makes known through reason and what he makes known through faith must cohere. Truth is truth, after all, and all of it is God's. So, how can one truth contradict another one? Truth is saying of what is that it is, conforming what is claimed to what is real. Two real things are both real, no contradiction. Thus, what is given through faith and what is given through reason cannot ever contradict one another. Being a Christian does not permit one to shelve the mind, for when God makes the saint he does not unmake the man. On the contrary, the central Christian truth is that God entered the world as a man; apparently, he thinks pretty highly of human nature.

So, what do we do when the truths of reason and the truths of faith appear to contradict one another? St. Thomas addresses this in the last lines of chapter

7. Since what God gives through faith and what God gives through reason cannot contradict one another, any natural argument that appears to oppose a truth of faith can confidently be countered by reason itself. Some mistake or misunderstanding had to have been made. It is the special province of bishops in the church to defend the faith against critics of this kind, and historically, you can find many volumes by the more famous of these Doctors of the Church who wrote "against" all kinds of heretical and opposing views (St. Augustine is a perfect example).

To sum up, St. Thomas sees no conflict between reason and faith, between thought and belief. On the contrary, true faith needs reason for its verification. Interesting, isn't it, how our first philosophical text, Plato's *Apology*, showed philosophy owing a debt to religion for its birth, and here we find our first theological text showing revealed religion needing philosophy for its account of authentic faith?

CHAPTER SIX

INOCULATION AGAINST CULT, PART 1

(John Locke, *Essay Concerning Human Understanding*, Bk. IV, Ch. 18)

John Locke is most famously known for his work opposing political tyranny. His are the ideas of natural right and the responsibility of governments to protect those rights. When governments not only fail to protect those rights, but even assault them, then people may resist and overthrow those governments. As Americans, we are pretty familiar with these ideas from Locke. But Locke also opposed two other kinds of tyranny in his work—philosophical tyranny and religious tyranny. We'll be interested in this latter category, and it will answer to something we've wondered about already: how can we distinguish authentic religion from a cult? Locke worries about this problem, too, because cults dominate people tyrannically, don't they? Cults seize your property, your cash, your freedom, your spouse, your kids, and ultimately your identity. But is all religion cult? Locke doesn't think so, but in order to precisely distinguish a cult from authentic religion, he thinks that we must understand faith.

Why is faith so important? Well, look what he says in the opening paragraphs of our text for today: how every religious group seems to lay claim to argument so long as it furthers their cause. But as soon as the going gets rough, you hear all about mystery, and how the ways of God are above the ways of man, and how that's where faith comes in. If every group can appeal to "faith" to justify whatever is difficult, then there's no way at all to adjudicate real faith from its imposter. Thus, sorting this out becomes our first objective.

Locke immediately moves toward the definitions of reason and of faith. So, let's begin with reason. Locke defines reason as that intellectual faculty which can discover truth through intuition, demonstration, or probability. Let's differentiate those three means of discovery. By "intuition" Locke does *not* mean our popular notion of something akin to a sixth sense, that intuitive feel you get that you are being watched. No, he means something strictly logical, namely reason's ability to discover first principles, what he calls self-evident propositions. An example? Take one of the fundamental laws of logic, the law of non-contradiction: a thing cannot both be and not be in the same way at the same time. Or, consider an instantiation of the law of identity: all brown dogs are brown. You see how in each case, as soon as you understand the meanings of the concepts involved, you right away realize that the proposition must be true? Such propositions do not need arguments to demonstrate them, but they do serve as premises in the demonstration of other truths. And that brings us to our second means of discovery, namely "demonstration." A proposition is demonstrated whenever it is proven from other propositions. Suppose that the premises, 1) All men are mortal, and 2) Socrates is a man, were true. What then would follow? Clearly 3) Socrates is mortal. The conclusion (3) is demonstrated from the premises (1-2). So long as the premises of a demonstration are known with certainty, the conclusion is likewise known with certainty. Thus, strict demonstrations and intuitions guarantee knowledge, which for Locke is certainty of truth.

That leaves us with probability. Reason infers propositions probabilistically in all those cases where the evidence does not warrant a necessary conclusion. Thus, imagine that you are looking at a pond full of swans, and you conclude from the twenty or so you've seen that all swans are white. That conclusion, while somewhat likely (i.e., probable) is nevertheless not guaranteed to be true, since you might not realize that in another lake there are blue swans. Of course, if you are a swan expert, and if you've examined all bodies of water on the earth, and *then* you conclude that all swans are white (having seen tens of thousands of swans), your conclusion that all swans are white is highly likely (i.e., very probable) though still not *guaranteed* to be true. It's still remotely possible that there is a blue swan somewhere that you happened to have missed. Thus, probability admits of degrees: we can be more or less confident of a probabilistic conclusion based on the amount and nature of the evidence before us. But probability does not confer certainty, and, thus, it is a weaker form of truth discovery than intuition and demonstration.

Locke next moves to identify the scope of reason, i.e., what are those things that reason can know or probabilistically discover? He offers us three classifications:

1. What is *according to reason*: any proposition the truth of which we can discover by examining and tracing those ideas we have from sensation and reflection and by natural deduction find to be true or probable

    Example: existence of myself or existence of God

2. What is *above reason*: any proposition whose truth or probability we cannot by reason derive from those principles

    Example: final resurrection of the dead; eternal life; original state of angels

3. What is *contrary to reason*: any proposition which is inconsistent with or irreconcilable to our clear and distinct ideas

<u>Example</u>: contradictions such as there is more than one supreme being, or that square circles exist

Of course, you'll realize that St. Thomas employed the same distinctions as Locke does, and, like St. Thomas, Locke thinks that reason and faith are perfectly complementary. Faith pertains to the reasonable acceptance of truths that are above reason, things for which reason is unsuitable to directly discover (for the simple reason that it lacks access to the relevant facts). No truth of faith could ever contradict reason, of course. In fact, reason places several important restrictions on faith, precisely because it is only through reason that appeals to faith can themselves be justified. Let's take a look at these now.

First, "No man inspired by God can by any revelation *communicate to others any new simple ideas* which they had not before from sensation or reflection" (Sect. 3). Locke means that if someone had a special vision from God that enabled him to experience wholly new kinds of experience (say, something akin to a brand new sense faculty), he would be unable to communicate the content of that experience to you, since the words he used would not refer to anything in your experience. St. Paul had an experience once in which he was briefly taken up into heaven, but he had no means to relate that experience to anyone else. People who have near death experiences often run into the same trouble.

Second, the same truths *may* be conveyed through revelation that are discoverable through reason, but, if known directly through reason, then they are *known* (rather than believed by faith). A great example might be a moral law, something so important that, though we can know it through reason, we might nevertheless also find that God inscribes it on two tablets of stone that he hands to Moses. But if you hadn't carefully considered the reason for that moral law and held it instead by faith, your confidence would not rise to the level of the certainty possessed by reason through demonstration or intuition.

Third, "no proposition can be received for divine revelation, or obtain the assent due to all such, if it be contradictory to our clear intuitive knowledge"—

therefore, philosophy and theology cannot conflict (Sect. 5). Now this one might surprise you, because here reason restricts the content of a theological revelation, and since earlier we admitted that reason cannot verify the content of revelations because it has no direct access to the information, this third rule might puzzle you. But Locke is not saying that reason can make a positive judgment as to the veracity of a revelation's content (say, e.g., that God is three in person and one in substance), but only that it can pass a negative judgment if anything within that revelation contradicts what is already known via intuition, i.e., a first principle known with certainty. Let's think about why this would have to be true on Locke's account.

Notice first of all, that our assurance that something is a revelation, say the doctrine of the trinity I mentioned above, is based on our confidence that the source of that revelation is reliable. Thus, if some fellow named Jesus tells me that he is a messenger from God, and he asks me to believe in the Holy Trinity, I might reasonably ask why I ought to believe that he is a messenger from God. The evidence he offers me will all be probabilistically reasonable, never demonstrably reasonable, since the kind of evidence that confirms that a person is an oracle of God is always empirical and historical, never possessing the kind of certainty as pure logic or mathematics. So, if the content of the revelation proved to be a contradiction (the only way to violate what is known in intuition), then that content would violate the most fundamental laws of logic which are held to be certainly true. Nothing held only probabilistically could ever oust something held certainly. Moreover, and secondly, the only way for me to infer that this Jesus really is a messenger from God is if I *reason* about the evidence he offers me, but if the laws of logic are what I'm asked to reject by the alleged message from God, then that revelation actually undermines the only way I can verify that it really is a revelation from God! I have to use logic to reason, don't I? So, it'd be as absurd as a prophet from God claiming to have a divine revelation that claims that there is no God. Self-contradictions are never true. What follows from this third point is a crucial principle: the claim of inspiration (i.e., the claim that one is a messenger from God) cannot itself ever be a matter of faith, or else we lose all ability to evaluate whether the revelation is real or fake. "*Nothing* that is contrary to and inconsistent with clear and self-evident dictates of reason, has a right to be urged or assented to as a matter of faith" (Sect. 10). Therefore, reason imposes an absolute limit on the content of faith. Of course, one had better take care about what counts as "known via intuition"! Locke doesn't mean current scientific theories, which are themselves only known probabilistically.

So, let's pull it all together, shall we? Locke thinks that faith is a species of reason, a special kind of reasoning that we actually use all the time. Any time I am asked to believe something based not on my own evaluation of the situation, but on the credit of the proposer, I'm being asked to use faith. Thus, if you saw Henry stab Janet, and I am a juror, I have to trust your testimony. Is that trust blind? No, of course not, as the prosecutor will try his best to show me that you are a reliable person. Naturally, Henry's attorney will try to prove that you are a lying wretch. Regardless of what turns out to be true, the issue is that we use evidence to try to evaluate not what you claim you saw (we weren't there) but whether you are an honest reporter of the facts. Religious faith works just like this. When an alleged messenger of God reports something that we cannot verify directly, we have to ask whether he really is a messenger of God. And we use reason to evaluate that.

Jesus offers us a beautiful example of this in one of the stories from the Gospels. At some point he comes upon a paralytic, and he says to him, "Your sins are forgiven" (Matthew 9:2). Now let's stop and analyze that claim. How could anyone, including the paralytic, evaluate whether his sins were forgiven or not? He wouldn't really know for sure until he died and stood before the divine judgment, so in the meantime, what is he to make of this claim? This is exactly how cult leaders act, don't they, making remarkable claims for which there is no possible evidence? And in both the case of the cult leader and Jesus we can reasonably ask how do we know that this message of forgiven sins is really true, is really from God. Well, Jesus is well aware of this problem (that's why he began by forgiving the man's sins), and in the story he waits a few moments for the significance of what he has said to sink in. His audience knows that only God can forgive sins, and, thus, they begin to suspect him of blasphemy. Who does this guy think he is, anyway? Once that's well set in their imaginations, Jesus then says the following, "But that you may know that the son of man (himself) has the authority to forgive sins, I say to you (the paralytic), rise up and walk" (Matthew 9:6). The man immediately stood up, his paralysis completely healed. Now, think hard about what Jesus just did. He vouched for his authority to forgive sins (i.e., his status as a divine messenger, as the Son of God) by offering evidence that he really was from God. What evidence? A supernatural effect, a miracle. Supernatural effects are caused by supernatural beings, aren't they? Thus, Jesus makes use of reason to vouch for his claim to be the Son of God. Locke would evaluate this story as a perfect example of how authentic faith is a species of reason.

For Locke it is proper to have faith in the content of a revelation only if you have good reason to believe that it really is a revelation, i.e., that the revealer is actually from God. But only reason can assess whether he is from God or not. If it were not this way, then we would be subject to every charlatan who came along claiming to represent God. And then we'd be subject to religious (or cult-like) tyranny.

CHAPTER SEVEN

INOCULATION AGAINST CULT, PART 2

(John Locke, *Essay Concerning Human Understanding*, Bk. IV, Ch. 19)

In our last chapter we saw Locke's positive development of his theory of faith and its relationship to reason. Locke argued that authentic faith depends upon reason, not to evaluate the truth of the message (which it cannot do, since the message surpasses the scope of reason), but, instead, to evaluate the veracity of the messenger. For no message from God could come to us unless it were presented to us by some prophetic person, a divine messenger. Thus, reason's job is to determine whether a person who claims to represent God really does so.

Of course, many people don't think of faith like this at all, do they? In this chapter, we will see Locke's attack on these opponents, what he calls the "enthusiasts." The Enthusiasts were the "leap-of-faithers" in Locke's time, people who thought of faith as opposed to reason, as a leap in the dark, against rationality. Locke thought it critical to examine their views, so that he could complete his defense of true faith against this false cousin that so easily misleads people into the most extravagant opinions and into the embrace of cult leaders.

He begins his argument by asking what has the right to command our assent, i.e., our beliefs. Think carefully about your answer. Locke says that only *truth* has the right to command assent, for the end (or aim) of belief is truth. Thus, I am allowed to believe things only to the degree that I have reason to think that they are true. Hence, love of truth is the first step in his argument. And of course, both philosophers and religious people claim to love the truth. Locke's worry is that though we *say* that, we nevertheless form many of our beliefs according to our interests rather than what is true. Sometimes what we want to be true has a way of sneaking into our minds as overly plausible. He calls this "belief according to inclination" (Sect. 1). But such a pragmatic approach undermines the point of belief, the goal of which is truth.

Lovers of truth have a duty then, both philosophical and religious, to use the system that God gave them, namely reason, for the assessment of claims to truth. Locke maintains the principle that when God makes the saint, he does not unmake the man. Grace never contradicts nature; it only fulfills it.

Locke next illustrates three possible grounds for assenting to a claim:

1. **Reason**: discovery of the certainty or probability of such propositions or truths, which the mind arrives at by deduction made from such ideas, which it has got by the use of its natural faculties.
2. **Faith**: assent to any proposition, not thus made out by the deductions of reason, but upon the *rationally verified credit* of the proposer, as coming from God, in some extraordinary way of communication. This way of discovering truths to men we call revelation.
3. **Enthusiasm**: assent to any proposition, not thus made out by the deductions of reason, but upon the *mere claims* of the proposer, as coming from God, in some extraordinary way of communication.

FAITH & REFLECTION

Now, you can probably see the vast difference between Locke's account of authentic faith on the one hand, and enthusiasm, on the other. In faith, reason assesses the veracity of the messenger, and only then accepts the content of the message. In enthusiasm we are asked to accept both the content of the message and the veracity of the messenger by "faith." So, imagine if I were to tell you that I am a prophet from God (didn't know that, did you?), and that I am now going to reveal a great truth to you. I tell you that if you eat three lollipops per day, then you will enter heaven! Now, let's further imagine that we are operating on the enthusiast's system. Then, when you ask me why you should believe my message, I will tell you that you must accept it by faith. And then when you ask me why you should believe that I am a messenger of God, I will tell you that you must accept that by faith too.

This puts you into a rather difficult position, doesn't it? For on this system, anyone can just claim to be a messenger from God based on whatever fancy he happens to believe. If he feels strongly about something, he might just start thinking that that feeling is caused by God, in which case, we must follow it. This kind of enthusiastic "faith" imposes very strongly upon us, because there is no possible way that we can evaluate it. And this is just what the enthusiast has in mind, doesn't he? Because he wants my submission to his religious authority. And that is religious tyranny, the origin of cult.

But why would anyone find enthusiasm attractive? Locke diagnoses the cause. Men are in love with their own opinions and find thrilling any system which suggests that whatever they happen to believe strongly is really divinely authorized. Moreover, enthusiasm appeals to men's laziness, because, without any hard intellectual work to mine the gems of truth from the nonsense that surrounds us, these men just "know!" Perhaps you can see the dangers that Locke fears for those that form beliefs according to their own inclinations rather than according to the love of the truth.

Locke offers four distinct arguments against the Enthusiasts' view of "faith." First, if this view were true, it would leave the faithful with no way to distinguish the true Spirit of God from an evil spirit, or even their own wishful thinking. In short, it would place us under the power of darkness with no ability to fulfill St. John's dictate that one "try the spirits to see whether they be of God" (I John 4:1).

Second, what do we do if two prophet-types both claim that they represent God, yet their messages conflict? If enthusiasm were true, and if self-confidence be taken as sufficient evidence that one is a prophet, then God would be the author of contradictory claims, but that would make God a liar. Thus, enthusiasm is not true.

Third, the enthusiast actually argues in a circle. The message in question is allegedly revelation because he firmly believes it. And he firmly believes it because he alleges that it is revelation! But that is just circular reasoning, begging the question, assuming what is supposed to be proven, and that never justifies anything.

Fourth, and finally, Locke points out that just being sincere is no test of truth, because well-intentioned people have proven to be wrong before. He cites the case of St. Paul who started out as a killer intent on crushing the new Christian faith. He was very devoted. But it was he, Locke asserts, and not the Christians who were in the wrong. Just because someone seems very sincere doesn't make him right.

Let's ask finally what would vouch for a prophetic message? What counts as sufficient evidence to warrant our believing that someone really is a messenger from God? Locke's answer: supernatural effects are evidence of supernatural origin. Thus, the messenger needs some kind of miraculous evidence to support his claim to prophetic status. Take the example of Moses as a case in point. There's Moses out in the wilderness chatting with God about how he is now supposed to represent the people of God (Israel) to the king of

Egypt and demand their immediate release from slavery. Moses points out to God that not only will the Egyptians reject him, his own people will laugh at him as some nut. God agrees with this assessment, and tells Moses to throw his stick on the ground, which he does. As it hits the earth, it turns into a snake. Moses nods, yes, that is impressive. Then God says to him, but if they don't believe this first sign, try this: put your hand in your shirt. Moses does so, and when he pulls it back out, it's leprous. Moses hastily returns it to the shirt, and it comes out good as new. And then God says, but if they don't accept the first two signs, try this one, and he enables him to turn water into blood, the first sign that he uses on the Egyptians. What's the upshot of all this? Locke thinks that God is well aware of the problem of sending someone to represent a divine message without backing his prophet with evidence that this guy really is from God. And so God supports Moses' status in triplicate. God does not impose upon human reason; rather, he expects us to use it. When God makes the saint, he does not unmake the man.

CHAPTER EIGHT

MIRACLES, PART 1

(John Locke, *Discourse of Miracles*)

In our last chapter we looked at Locke's critique of his major opponents on faith, the enthusiasts. The enthusiasts believed that faith was an anti-rational acceptance of divine truth. Enthusiasts usually have one of two reasons for thinking that their method is sensible. First, they sometimes argue that God is just too far beyond human beings for reason to be useful in understanding him. But if that were true, then no message from God whether derived from faith or enthusiasm would be the least bit understandable. So, this argument is too strong. Second, they sometimes argue that, okay, God isn't the problem, we are. Maybe our reasoning is so flawed, so fallen, that we just cannot use it to reason about these matters. Why would God leave something as important as divine truth to a system as fallible as human reason? This argument might appear to make more sense than the last one, but let's examine it a little bit. Even if this were true, wouldn't we still have to use reason to *understand* what is said in the revelation, the meanings of the words? At some point the revelation must be presented to us in a way that reason has to be used. Reason is all we've got. Granted, we do sometimes make mistakes with it, but the answer isn't to give up reasoning and believe whatever anyone else says, but to refine and hone our reasoning through education, so that we can form more accurate beliefs.

Locke's theory of faith depends upon some kind of supernatural signs that the messenger really is from God. These signs are called miracles. So, it behooves us to examine miracles. What are they? How do they occur? Would we ever be justified in believing in them?

Fortunately, Locke begins with a precise definition of a miracle. A miracle is an event which seems to the spectator to be outside the usual course of nature, beyond what he takes to be a natural physical law. You might be surprised at the apparent spectator-dependence of a miracle. Surely, we should define a miracle as an event that violates a natural law. But Locke thinks that such a definition is highly problematic, because what if we've misunderstood the natural laws? Then God might do something truly astounding, say at the quantum level, and because our physics hasn't moved beyond the 15th century, we'd be wholly unable to identify the event as miraculous. Thus, an event will be significant to someone only if it exceeds *his* understanding of what is normal.

Okay, so that does make sense. But then Locke seems faced with another really big problem: lots of events that aren't miracles might be mistaken for miracles! Locke is ready for this too, however, and yes, he admits, that is true. But it won't prove problematic for several important reasons, and he spends the rest of the discourse offering these reasons.

First, Locke asks us to consider what *kind* of miracles we're concerned with, and he explains that we're interested only in what he calls an *attestation* miracle, i.e., a miracle offered to vouch for a prophetic claim, a sign designed to vouch for someone that he really is delivering a divine message. There may be all kinds of additional events that occur throughout history that may or may not be miracles. Our inability to sort all of these out is beside the point, because we're interested only in a special kind of miracle, that kind of miracle which is used to support a revelatory claim.

Second, Locke points out that ancient paganism never used attestation miracles, because their deities never claimed supremacy over everyone else nor offered a universal message. Only monotheism makes this supremacy claim. So, miracles alleged to have occurred in pagan cultures don't matter at all. Maybe they happened, maybe they didn't; maybe people had trouble telling whether those strange events were miracles or oddities of nature . . . it doesn't concern us here. Our issue is the attestation miracles, and they never occur in pagan religion.

Third, of the monotheistic religions, only three offer special revelation in the form of special messages communicated to men from God. They include Judaism, Christianity, and Islam. But of these three, Islam offers no attestation miracles, but claims that the Koran is itself the miracle, i.e., that the message is the sign that the message is divine. But that isn't an attestation miracle at all. Mohammed offers nothing to vouch for his prophetic claim. So, we're left with Judaism and Christianity. And since Christians see Judaism as their intellectual and spiritual ancestor, Locke sees no competition between them, but a deep complementarity.

Now, even within Christianity and Judaism, we really only find major attestation miracles associated with two hugely significant events, namely the giving of the Law to Moses and the giving of the Son of God to the world in the Incarnation. So, were Jesus and Moses actual messengers from God or not? Locke argues that if they are, then they'd better have attestation miracles to back them up, and enough of them to overcome the possible mistakes that people might make in confusing miraculous events with non-miraculous events.

And, so, we come to Locke's "cluster" theory of the attestation miracles. Imagine you are a Jew during the second temple period and you hear about this teacher, Jesus of Nazareth. You hear someone report that he actually saw Jesus walk on water. Now, this guy has been your neighbor for all your life and always seemed pretty honest. But you don't find this miraculous, because maybe Jesus was just turtle-hopping. Okay, that event doesn't do it for you. Then what about when he calmed the stormy sea with a word? Well, you mull that one over and admit it is more interesting, but still, maybe since his friends were all seasoned fishermen, that they indicated that the storm was just about to break, and then he "calmed" the sea. Fair enough, but someone else might well find that event miraculous. But you don't. Okay, then what about when Jesus healed the sick from dawn until dusk, thousands of people, all of their ailments. Nothing like the tent evangelist who "heals" people for whom there's little evidence of real sickness. Rather, imagine someone walking through a modern hospital and instantaneously completely healing every single person who was ill. Mulling that one over, you might conclude, okay, there is something strange going on here . . .

That's how Locke thinks the cluster effect works. What one person doesn't take as a miracle, another person will, and on and on. If God expects us to believe that this person really is a messenger from God, then he needs to vouch for his messenger. And in both the case of Moses and Jesus we find huge clusters of miracles. If you were an Israelite watching Moses's little signs, and then watching the ten plagues, and then watching the Red Sea open up for your people (when Moses raised his stick), and then watching that same sea come crashing down on your Egyptian pursuers (again when Moses raised his stick), and then watched the whole thunder and lightning and mountain shaking at Mount Sinai, and then watched the manna fall from heaven every single day . . . at some point would it be so irrational of you to believe that, yes, this Moses guy really is a messenger from God, and maybe we'd better listen to him?

Okay, so Locke has dealt with the problem of people disagreeing about whether something really was a miracle. At some point, he thinks you'll find something impressive in what Jesus does. Even his enemies in the Gospels finally admit that they cannot deny the miracles, so they decide to attribute them to the devil. But of course Jesus' miracles are (with the one exception of the cursed fig tree) all good events, restoring things according to nature. So, if Jesus is working for the devil, it's rather bizarre that his teaching aims men at God and his miracles direct events toward divine peace. So, Jesus says to his critics that a house divided against itself cannot stand: how can the devil be working against the devil? In other words, he's truly representing God.

But maybe now we do have a point to raise against Locke, since Jesus brought up this issue of rival miracles. What if another alleged prophet stood up and did counter-miracles against the prophet of God all the while denying everything the true prophet said? How would miracles help us sort this problem out?

Well, that's a great question, but Locke is prepared to handle this worry too, and again he refers us to the miracle cluster events, where just such a situation occurred. Going back to the Moses case, if you read the text of Exodus carefully, you'll notice that the Pharaoh's sorcerers actually duplicated Moses' first four plague miracles. And when Moses first showed up in Pharaoh's court and did the staff-to-snake conversion, the sorcerers dropped their sticks and they all turned into snakes too. Fortunately, the text of Exodus also gives us an idea of what was really going on here. God explains to Moses that he intends to gain glory against the gods of Egypt. In other words, God himself has upstart rivals in the Egyptian deities, and God intends to show them who is boss. So, the sorcerers of Egypt served real gods, what Christians came to call demons (the term 'god' simply refers to any being who is a spirit, i.e., not embodied by nature), so it wasn't surprising that they should back their priests with real powers.

This is just the kind of case we were imagining would pose a difficulty for Locke's theory, right? Rival claims backed by rival miracles. Well, Locke points us to the rest of the story. First, when the sorcerers dropped their staffs and they all turned into snakes, the snake of Moses devoured all of them. And second, the sorcerers were only able to duplicate the first four plagues; after that, they were mystified. Moses' power exceeded their power.

So, it seems that Locke is arguing that greater power proves which messenger is authentic. But then it could appear that Locke is saying that might makes right. But Locke is actually arguing the reverse, namely that right makes might. Since God is omnipotent (infinitely powerful), then he must back his messenger with the greater display of power, so that greater power does indicate the real prophet. Otherwise, God is a deceiver, for we have no other appeal except to his own nature. But God is not a deceiver, so where he puts forward a messenger who meets a rival and we get a miraculous showdown, God must and will back his prophet with superior signs of power.

We see a similar strategy at work in the story of Elijah facing off against the prophets of Baal. In this case, Elijah challenges the false prophets to a test. Let each side build an altar and let each side pray to his god, and may the real god send down fire from heaven to consume the sacrifice. Then Elijah gives the Baal prophets the first go, so they spend the next six hours begging their god to send down fire from heaven. They dance, they sing, they cut themselves, and they even have to endure Elijah mocking them ("maybe you should shout louder, because your god may be off on vacation"), but nothing happens to their altar. Finally, Elijah has had enough, so he calls for multiple barrels of water to pour over his altar, so much that it fills a trench around the base. He is determined to make clear that he's not cheating in any way. Then he says a quick prayer to God and, sure enough, fire comes down and consumes not only the sacrifice, but the entire altar as well. The people of Israel are impressed and come over to Elijah's side.

Let's summarize Locke's position in closing. First, attestation miracles are those events offered as support of a prophet/messenger of God to vouch for him that he really does represent God. Such events are miracles only if they appear to the spectator to be supernatural, outside the usual course of nature. Only then will the spectator believe it reasonable to infer that the supernatural event was caused by a supernatural being, namely God. Second, attestation miracles occur only in the two monotheistic religions and occur in clusters only in the central cases of the giving of the Mosaic Law and in the Incarnation. Because they occur in clusters, spectators' varying degrees of experience and skepticism can all be satisfied. Third, in the case of rival miracles backing rival messages, since God is backing his own messenger, he must on pain of deception, support his own messenger with greater power.

Let's look at one last case from the Hebrew Bible which illustrates Locke's point nicely. An Israelite named Gideon is minding his own business one day when he is called out by God to raise an army and throw off an oppressor. Gideon wonders if he's losing his mind, hearing voices. So, he asks the voice, "Okay, if you are really God, then prove it by tomorrow morning when the dew falls on the grass, let this sheep skin come out completely dry." Sure enough, the next morning the sheep skin is dry. But then Gideon wonders, "Hmm . . . that actually wasn't so difficult. Anybody might have come by and dropped a dry sheep skin down." So, he goes back to the voice and says, "All right, that was pretty good, but let's have another go at this. This time, make the grass all dry and make only the sheep skin covered in dew." Sure enough, the next morning, the dew lies only on the sheep skin. Gideon accepts his divine commission.

CHAPTER NINE

MIRACLES, PART 2

(David Hume, *Enquiry Concerning Human Understanding*, "Miracles")

We've been reading Locke's work on faith, and we've seen that he thinks that faith must be grounded in evidence that the messenger of the word of God is really authentic. And only evidence of a supernatural nature can pull that off. So, miracles are essential to divine revelation, and, thus, to faith. We then examined Locke's definition and account of how miracles work if they really do occur.

But David Hume thought that there were some problems in Locke's account, first as to the definition of a miracle, and, second, as to whether we can really possess any confidence that they occur. Let's start with Hume's alternative definition of a miracle. Hume suggests that a miracle is a violation of a natural law. Now, most people who offer their unreflective definition of a miracle would probably say something like this. You'll recall, though, that Locke made a miracle spectator-dependent; otherwise, it might not even be recognized. Hume never addresses the value of spectator-dependency.

Hume proceeds to launch two attacks on what he takes miracles to be. Let's begin with his definitional, or, *semantic* attack. Hume notes that a natural law is a principle drawn from unexceptionable experience. Were there even one exception, we'd not classify the hypothesis as a natural law. So, nothing can act contrary to a natural law. But what about miracles, we might ask? Well, if an event really did act contrary to a natural law, then Hume thinks we'd better conclude that what we thought was a natural law really wasn't. And then our "miracle" loses all significance, because these events are interesting only if they stand out against our experience. Thus, no miracle can occur, on pain of contradiction, since a miracle is an event that is purported both to occur and, at the same time, to violate a rule (a natural law) that says that they never, ever occur.

This argument of Hume's hasn't fared very well against the critics, however, since many people worry that he's simply defined himself into being right. Given his definitions, yes, no miracles ever could occur, but why grant this definition? Locke certainly didn't. What's more, should we even grant his supposition that events are significant only if they violate natural laws?

So, Hume moves on to his second attack on miracles, what we might call the evidential, or, *epistemic* attack. This time, Hume argues that, okay, maybe a miracle might occur, but you'd never have any reason to believe that it did. Why? Because it's always more likely that you are seeing things or out of your mind (both of which have happened in the history of human events) than that you really did witness a miracle (which has never happened before). Now, lest you object that surely this rule is too restrictive, because it would rule out all new experience, Hume is ready for this. He talks of the Indian prince who is told about the existence of ice, hard water. Surely the prince would rightly be skeptical of such a report. But, of course, he at least can check for himself, and if enough people report that ice is real, then how insane can he be?

But are we so sure that these same moves might not likewise apply in the miracle case? If Jesus is reported as a miracle worker, I can check for myself. And Hume's criticism remains against both the Indian prince case and the Jesus case, for in both cases, while I check for myself, might I not be crazy (which has happened before)? And if Hume retorts, "But in the ice case other people witness the event," the same thing is true of many of Jesus' miracles. And to again push Hume's reasoning, don't mass hallucinations occur? So, shouldn't I reject either both ice and Jesus' miracles, or neither? Is there really a difference between a new event and a miracle on Hume's accounting? Maybe his argument is too strong, ruling out far more than he really means to.

We can approach the epistemic argument against miracles in another way too, if we imagine that one of us reports having seen someone rise from the dead last night. We can all say that that person is nuts, on drugs, grossly mentally unbalanced, etc., and thus write him off. But then let's suppose that another one of us comes the next day and says the same thing. Well, again, let's apply Hume's logic: it's more likely that that person, too, is nuts rather than that miracles occur, because, while miracles have never happened before, people have gone insane. Okay, but then what happens if the next day *you* see the resurrection and come to us and report, yep, I saw it too. Is it still reasonable for us to continue to reject your report? But on Hume's logic, how can we admit the miracle? We could continue this through every member of our town until we conclude that we're all nuts, we can't trust what we plainly just saw, and still Hume's logic holds.

So, if this little example convinces you that something is amiss, let's try to figure out what it is. In each case, Hume told us that it's more likely that we're nuts (which has happened before) than that a miracle occurred (which has never happened before). Let's examine that claim. In his famous critique of Hume's argument in *Miracles*, C. S. Lewis asks how do we know that a miracle has never happened before? Presumably because no one has ever reported one, right? But is that true? Isn't it in fact true that each person that reports a miracle is written off, right out of the evidence pool, because we assume he must be nuts? But of course, this begs the question, doesn't it? It's not that we know a miracle has never happened before; it's rather that we reject any reports of miracles because we are presuming that they never happen, presuming without evidence. But we're supposed to be proving that it is unreasonable to believe in miracles. Instead, it turns out we are assuming that it's unreasonable to believe in miracles. This is arguing in a circle, begging the question.

Of course, if we check history, we'll find voluminous reports of miracles, and in the cases that Locke referred us to, the attestation miracles surrounding Moses and Jesus, we have many reports. So, it's not true that there are no prior reports. But even if there weren't, are we really prepared to say that we know the universe so well, that we can say what cannot ever happen on pain of contradiction (in the semantic attack) or on pain of insanity (in the epistemic attack)? Who's being the dogmatist here?

Consider: let's suppose that God existed and wished to communicate with men in the divine revelation way that Locke describes. What could he do in principle to convince us that he is real and is trying to get our attention? On Hume's argument, there is nothing he could possibly do, because, in each case, we could write off the evidence, even to the point of saying that we're insane. But can we really just declare that the spiritual realm is false? What if God and the angels and demons really exist? What if ghosts and the paranormal are real? Couldn't they break through into our world, showing real effects and intentionality, to convince us of their reality? Can we say in principle that it's always irrational to believe this, in spite of the evidence? What kind of rationality rejects all evidence?

CHAPTER TEN

THE COSMOLOGICAL ARGUMENT

(David Hume, *Dialogues Concerning Natural Religion*, Part IX)

Thus far in this book we've been examining the **epistemology** of religion and inquiry. Epistemology is the theory of knowledge. We've been concerned with evaluating the rival philosophical and religious claims that have been made throughout history and which have sometimes been responsible for cultic entrapments. We've learned how reason can function both philosophically and religiously to act as a kind of inoculation against cultic tyranny, separating faith from the "mere fancies of a man's brain" (to use Locke's quip).

We're now going to move to the **metaphysics** of religion. If you go to your local book store and check out the "metaphysics" section, you are likely to find all sorts of books on the new age, occult, pyramid forces, crystals, and the like. But would you believe that these new age folks actually hijacked the term "metaphysics" from us, the philosophers? It was Aristotle (Plato's prize student) who first coined the term. It means the study of what is. Metaphysics is the science of reality itself, the ultimate natures of things. So, if we ask about the metaphysics of religion, we mean to ask what religious objects exist, and if they do exist, what they are like. Examples? God, angels, demons, ghosts, heaven, hell, nirvana, purgatory, etc. The question is this: what can philosophy tell us about these objects? In today's chapter, we are going to discuss the existence of God. In the three chapters following, we'll look at his divine nature.

In his famous letter to the Christians in Rome, St. Paul says something that many people miss, namely that the knowledge of the existence of God is not held by faith, but by reason. He argues in Romans 1:19ff that the knowledge of God's nature (goodness) and eternal power are clearly seen from the evidence of what has been made. In other words, St. Paul argues from effect to cause, that something(s) about the nature of the creation tells us important information about the existence and nature of the cause, God.

Almost all (there is one exception, called the Ontological Argument) of the arguments for the existence of God follow the pattern St. Paul indicates. They pick some feature of the world and find the world itself insufficient to explain that feature. So, for example, some people make an argument from goodness, namely that goodness needs a ground outside of this world for its explanation. Others make an argument from beauty along the same lines, or perhaps, from purpose/function. But there's one of these kinds of arguments that argues for the existence of God from the general existence of anything whatsoever, so that in this argument's case, existence itself needs explanation.

You've probably asked the question yourself: if I was caused by my parents, and they by theirs, and on and on . . . does that sequence of causes and effects go on infinitely, or does it have a real start—a first cause? This argument, sometimes called the First Cause argument, but also by the better known name, the Cosmological Argument, starts with the world (the cosmos) and argues that it requires a divine explanation.

Now, scientifically, we might be able to make probabilistic arguments for God's existence given the nature of the universe as we currently understand it. For example, as we move back through universal history, we run into the starting event, the Big Bang, as it's been called. Yet we find ourselves driven to ask the question, "And what caused that?" To this, the scientists have no answer because all of the data points back to the bang itself, not to whatever caused it. So, many theists (believers in God's existence) think that this is the moment of creation. Indeed, if God does exist, then the evidence available to us in this universe definitely points to that being the moment of origin. But while this argument makes God's existence probable, there might yet be something else that accounts for the Big Bang.

The Cosmological Argument works very differently from the probabilistic argument I just offered from the Big Bang. It promises not probability, but certainty. In other words, if the Cosmological Argument works, then God's existence is necessary, given the existence of anything else. So, this promises to be an exciting argument!

How then does the Cosmological Argument work? Well, in our reading from Hume's *Dialogues Concerning Natural Religion*, you will notice Demea's presentation of the argument, that the sequence of past causes and effects either keeps going on forever or it had a first cause (or reason). So, the general structure of the argument is a dilemma: whether the universe goes back to a first event or goes on forever in past time, either way, God exists. To prove that God exists, then, we must first understand why the two lemmas are true: first, if the universe goes back to a first event, then God exists; and second, if the universe goes on forever in past time, God exists. So, let's start with the first lemma. (Two lemmas together are called a *dilemma* in logic. Demea's argument attempts to create such a dilemma in order to show that either way, God must exist. Notice that our popular use of the term "dilemma" as a tough problem to escape arises loosely from this stricter philosophical usage.)

Demea begins the argument with the assertion that everything that exists has a cause or a reason. Things exist either dependently on something else, or else they exist independently of anything else. If they exist independently of anything else, then we need to understand why (the reason) this is true. So, if the universe goes back in time to a first event, say the Big Bang, we then ask the question what caused that. The same process of reasoning that drove us back to the Big Bang can naturally be pressed against the Big Bang itself. The greatest explosion ever has to have arisen from something capable of producing it, so what was that thing?

Well, if the Big Bang is the *first* event, then it must have been caused by something that is not itself caused by anything else, i.e., a being whose existence does not need a cause. But what kind of being could not have a cause? To answer this question, we have to consider the nature of causation. If x causes y, then x must possess the resources to produce y. So, if I say that I single-handedly produced the Space Shuttle, you'll find that dubious, because you rightly suspect that my mind is insufficiently grand to hold the whole of the intricacies of the space shuttle! I lack the resources to produce the effect, so I cannot be its cause.

Now, let's apply this general rule to any particular finite being. We can see that it could have been produced by a greater finite being. So, every finite being could have a cause. So, let's switch to infinite beings (understood qualitatively, not quantitatively). Could a being that is infinite have a cause? Well, it would have to be produced by something equal to or greater than itself. But it cannot have been produced by something greater than itself, because an infinite being is infinitely powerful and there's nothing greater. So, could it have been produced by something exactly like itself? Well, here again, we run into a problem: can a universe exist with two omnipotent beings in it? Wouldn't their rival claims to supremacy cancel one or the other out? Yes, so there cannot be more than one Supreme Being (the definition of "supreme" is another way to see this).

So, what do we learn from this evaluation of causation? Any finite being can be caused, is dependent on something else for its existence. So, if the thing that produced the Big Bang is finite, the regress resumes and the Big Bang isn't the first event after all. But we stipulated (for this lemma) that it was the first event! So, the thing that produced it cannot be finite, but must be infinite, for only in that way will the regress not restart. Only infinite beings cannot have causes. There is no cause of God. But there is a reason for his existence, namely his own omnipotence, which is another way of stating that his existence is independent. Thus, God's existence is of a different type than ours. Ours is dependent, contingent on whatever produced us. But God's existence is independent and, thus, not contingent on anything else. His existence is necessary.

Let's return to the dilemma now. We said that if there is a finite regress then God must exist. But what about the other possibility, that there is an infinite regress? First of all, let's clear up what we're saying here, not that we know that there is an infinite regress of past time, since, obviously, all of our scientific data shows that the universe is finite, begun in time at the Big Bang. Rather, what we're saying is regardless of the scientific findings, it's still possible that it's infinitely past in a way for which we don't possess evidence, i.e., that the thing that started the Big Bang is finite after all but completely inaccessible to us. Then the regress could keep going. So, in that case, why would God have to exist?

Demea poses an interesting couple of questions about this possible infinite sequence of causes and effects. What explains why this universe exists as opposed to some other one, say the Tolkien universe or the Bugs Bunny or Star Trek universes? There's nothing incoherent about them, yet they don't exist and we do . . . why? Or we can ask the question the other way that Demea poses it: why does anything at all exist, as opposed to nothing at all? These two kinds of questions remain, meaning that our infinite regress of causes and effects still has some answers to provide. If the answers are contained within the regress, then those causes will just be sucked into the regress and the question can be reposed of the new whole. So, there must be some reason for this regress. Demea adds that it cannot be chance, nor can it be nothing, so what is that something that explains it? Answer: something that carries the reason for its existence within itself. And what is that? As we've already seen, God. Therefore, whether the universe has a finite beginning or goes on infinitely into the past, God exists.

Now, Demea's critics, Cleanthes and Philo, launch into six objections to Demea's argument. Cleanthes offers the first five, and he begins with an objection that he takes to be "entirely decisive," so it pays for us to consider it closely. To render it more accessible, I'm going to lay it out in standard form:

1. If something is conceivable as existing, then it is likewise conceivable as not existing (Assumption).
2. Any being is conceivable as existing (Assumption).
3. Therefore, any being is conceivable as not existing (1, 2).
4. If something is distinctly conceivable, it does not imply a contradiction (Def. of Contradiction)
5. Therefore, there is no being whose **non-existence** implies a contradiction (3, 4)
6. If something is demonstrable *a priori*, then its **negation does** imply a contradiction (Def. of *A priori* demonstration).
7. Therefore, there is no being whose **existence** is demonstrable *a priori* (5, 6).

To understand what Cleanthes is saying, we need to understand what it means to "demonstrate something *a priori*." Philosophers say that we can know things dependent on experience (*a posteriori*) or independently of experience (*a priori*). Take the claim that brown dogs chase cats. You would not know that this were true, unless you went out and examined brown dogs. Thus, if you knew this claim, you'd know it *a posteriori*, based on experience. But now consider the following claim: all brown dogs are brown. You don't need to go out and check, do you? You know this as soon as you understand what is being said, independently of checking experientially. You know this *a priori*. Notice that if you deny that all brown dogs are brown, that you get a contradiction. Cleanthes is arguing that because any being is conceivable as either existing or not existing (i.e., you *don't* get a contradiction from denying its existence), then no being's existence can be necessary and, thereby, demonstrable *a priori*.

Well, you might wonder about this argument, and there's a good reason. Ask yourself whether the first premise could be true *if the Cosmological argument's conclusion were true*. I mean, if God's existence necessarily follows from the existence of anything else, then can you conceive of God as either existing or as not existing? If the Cosmological Argument worked, then you'd not be able to conceive of God's non-existence any more than you could maintain that not all brown dogs are brown. What's the point? Cleanthes has assumed what he was supposed to prove. His first premise denies the conclusion of his opponent's argument, and that's called begging the question, or arguing in a circle. Bad beginning, but maybe his other arguments will prove better?

In his second argument Cleanthes objects to the notion of "necessary existence" itself, saying that it applies solely to propositions, not to things. So, while a proposition such as "2+2=4" can be necessarily true, no being can be necessarily existent. But this argument isn't really a decent argument either, is it? For if the Cosmological Argument works, necessity does apply to things too. This is another question-begging argument.

Let's move to his third objection. Cleanthes asks an intriguing question: why couldn't the property of necessary existence apply to the universe itself? If this were true, we'd not need God in the system. So, whether the universe is finite or infinite, maybe it is itself the "necessarily existent thing." We've finally got a real objection, so let's take a look at it and see if it's cogent.

Could the material universe, matter, be the necessarily existent thing? We say sometimes in physics that matter is neither created nor destroyed. But that's not really the same thing, is it? We're asking about whether matter has to exist at all. Does it? Well, what feature of matter entails its existence? And can't we ask the question Demea asked of the universe all over again? Why this universe as opposed to another? Moreover, if matter is necessarily existent, then we run into a huge problem, namely that since matter is distinct and, thus, infinitely large in number, we end up with a vast number of necessarily existent, or, omnipotent things. But we've already argued that omnipotence cannot be the property of any more than one thing. So, not all matter can be independently/omnipotently existing.

Okay, so let's suppose that it's just one piece of matter that is the necessarily existent thing that explains the whole of the universe. Then we could cite its existence and dispense with God. But I wonder if perhaps we haven't deceived ourselves in calling this omnipotent piece of matter "matter." For if we have already given this thing the central divine attribute (omnipotence), isn't this piece of matter none other than God himself? We've just erroneously called him "matter."

So, that third argument of Cleanthes which seemed potent at first (at least it didn't beg the question) turns out upon analysis to return him to the original problem, right back into Demea's argument. So, let's move to the fourth objection. How can anything that is part of an infinite regress have a first cause? It cannot be first, if the regress goes back infinitely! So, all this talk of a first cause of an infinite regress is senseless.

It doesn't take much reflection on this argument to realize that Cleanthes is straw manning Demea. A "straw man" attack occurs where you attack not the person's real view, but a fake, a scare crow caricature, of the real view. How is

Cleanthes doing that here? Well, Demea's first premise was that everything has a cause or a reason, not that everything has a cause. Nor did Demea ever say that God was the cause of the infinite regress, but, instead, that God's creative act was its reason. So, Cleanthes changes Demea's view, overly restricts it, and then attacks it for being overly restrictive.

This leaves us with one last argument from Cleanthes. Banking on the possibility of an infinite past regress (and, yes, if you worry whether that's even possible, Aristotle and St. Thomas Aquinas thought that it was definitely impossible, but we'll conditionally admit its possibility for our purposes here), Cleanthes asks why if he's already given an explanation for each event within the regress he should nevertheless have to give an explanation (a reason) of the whole? A whole collection of things isn't itself a thing, and, thus, it shouldn't require an explanation. Bertrand Russell, an early 20th century philosopher, said it this way, "Does the set of all mothers need a mother?" Sets are arbitrary collections fabricated by our minds, and they don't need explanations like this.

Well, let's mull that over. Might Cleanthes and Russell have a point? Are we making a big mistake here, shifting from asking about the explanation of things and then surreptitiously shifting to asking about the explanation of sets? To see if Cleanthes and Russell might be right, let's go back to the two questions Demea posed: why does anything exist at all? Why this universe as opposed to another one? Are these really set questions? Or are they questions about the members of the set, namely that nothing within the set is able to answer fundamental questions? Demea's point isn't about the "set" but about the fact that the members of the set cannot explain their existence. So, perhaps Cleanthes (and Russell) have moved us away from the real driving issue.

We have just one last argument, this time from Philo (hard work, isn't this?). Philo suggests that maybe everything is necessary, so that the property of necessary existence may not be particularly unique of God, nor do we need God to explain things. Moreover, if everything is necessary, then, in effect, determinism is true, and this hardly seems fitting for religion. So, maybe it'd be better for us never to have started talking about necessary existence at all. What do you think of this argument? Pull together everything that we've discussed in this chapter so far, and construct your own reply to Philo.

CHAPTER ELEVEN

THE DIVINE NATURE: OMNIPOTENT POWER

(C. S. Lewis, *Problem of Pain*, Ch. 2)

In our last chapter, we looked at one of the most famous proofs for the existence of God, and we learned something about God's nature too, namely the *kind* of power he possesses to be capable of independent existence: infinite or omnipotent power. In this chapter we want to think more about God's nature. We'll talk about God's power now, and in our next two chapters, we'll talk about God's goodness and love.

Now, before we dive into the metaphysics of divine power, let's consider the theological tradition for a moment, for philosophers are not the first to have considered the divine nature in this way! Think back to the evolution of the understanding of God in the Hebrew Bible. Let's start with Abraham. Abraham is called to a new land by God, but he doesn't know very much about God, does he? Why do I say this? Because his family packs all their idols with them as they travel! There doesn't seem to be any supremacy or exclusivity in this God's demands on Abraham. For all Abraham knows, maybe this God is just a Palestinian deity.

But when Abraham gets to Palestine, the king and high priest of Salem marches out to meet him. The Bible calls him Melchizedek and classifies him as a priest of the "most high God." Now, this is an intriguing development. The God who called Abraham out of Ur is not just another of the many gods. No, he is the top God, the most high. But notice that this understanding of God doesn't entail omnipotent supremacy either, because many of the pagan religions had a top god (like Zeus, e.g.) who became powerful by overcoming his predecessors (the Titans, in Zeus' case). So, maybe the God of Melchizedek is "most high" in that sense, or maybe he is the most high intrinsically (in the omnipotent sense). The texts don't tell us. Yet.

Let's move ahead in Israelite history a bit to get to Moses. Moses is marching around the desert with his sheep, and he encounters the famous burning bush. The voice calls out to him to remove his shoes for he is standing on holy ground. The voice then announces its identity, "I am" (Exodus 3:14). Well, that's a funny name. What about George, or Betsy, or Athena, or Apophis? But no, that's not what Moses gets. Notice that in this case God is naming himself, and note further that names reveal essences in the Hebrew Bible. So, this name of God reveals God's own nature. Here's where our philosophical skill has to kick in. What does this name *mean*? In other words, what is the nature of God?

Let's start with the verb, "am." We know that it is the present form of the verb "to be." Thus, God is stating that he is being itself, reality itself. He exists according to his own nature, his own essence. His existence is independent, intrinsic to himself. He is supreme, in other words, omnipotent. Here for the first time in the history of the world we get an absolutely clear indication of the idea of the supreme God, a God whose existence is incompatible with the existence of any other infinite being (though definitely compatible with the finite spirits/gods). Moreover, God calls himself an "I" meaning that he is particular, not just universal! So, God isn't everything, nor is everything God.

God is a definite I, distinct from you and distinct from me. Nevertheless, he possesses within himself maximal reality. Moreover, God isn't a thing but a person, a person who is at once full universality, maximal being, and complete perfection. He differs in kind from all of us, for who of us can say that our very nature is to exist? Our existence is dependent on something else, ultimately, on him. So, we say of God that he creates, while we are the created. None of the pagan deities possessed this status, for they were part of an already existing world. For the pagans, the world was a great womb out of which sprang the gods. But for the Jews, God's supremacy renders that conception impossible. What explains the world itself? Answer: God, who created it in the first place.

So, the theological tradition squares with the philosophical, doesn't it? Here again we find a remarkable parity between them. But of course, the philosophical tradition also tells us that the unexamined life is not worth living. So, let's begin to examine this feature of God, his divine power. We say of God that he can do anything. But what about making a rock too heavy for him to lift? If he can't do it, then he seems weak, and thus not omnipotent. If he can do it, then he can't lift the rock, and again, he seems weak, and thus not omnipotent. So, whether he can do it, or not, how can he be omnipotent? Is omnipotence something coherent?

This question about the rock too heavy for God to lift is an example of what is called an omnipotence paradox. A paradox is an apparent contradiction, what appears to be contradictory. If you can resolve it, then you show how the paradox might seem that way, but, upon analysis, doesn't in fact turn out that way. Before moving toward that analysis, let's consider another omnipotence paradox.

Can God commit suicide? If he can, then God can be killed, and that sounds like a contradiction, since a necessary being has to be necessary. If he can't, then again, God cannot do something, impinging his omnipotence.

In order to evaluate these paradoxes, C. S. Lewis asks us to think more carefully about what we mean when we say that God can do the impossible. Surely, he says, God can do the physically impossible, for what is physically impossible is impossible only because conditions are the way they are. If they had been otherwise, then the event wouldn't be impossible. Consider: I wish to jump to the moon. You will point out that my legs are insufficiently strong to jump that far. So, it is physically impossible for me to jump to the moon. But were my legs far greater . . . it wouldn't be physically impossible. So, Lewis classifies this kind of impossibility as conditional impossibility. The event in question is impossible assuming all the physical conditions are the same. When we say that God can do the impossible, we definitely mean to include the physically impossible, because God can just alter the conditions. So, it is physically impossible for water to be blown up on two sides of a marching column of people and held there until their pursuers chase them, and then fall down only on the pursuers. Quite right, but God can do the physically impossible, because he can alter all the physical conditions and enable the water to hold there. So, what is physically impossible (conditionally impossible), is not absolutely impossible.

This brings us to consider what is meant by "absolute" impossibility. Lewis offers this definition: what is absolutely impossible is that which is unconditionally impossible. In other words, no matter how much you alter the conditions in the situation, it cannot be done. Absolute impossibility properly describes only logical contradictions. Take a square circle, for example. Can a square circle exist? No. Okay, but is it merely physically impossible? Could we alter some condition so that in a different world square circles could exist? Again, you'll reply no. And you'd be right. Why? Because the square circle rules itself out, regardless of whatever universe you try to place it in. The concepts of square and circle are mutually excluding. Nothing can be both. If you try to imagine a square circle, you'll either get a rounded square, or an edged circular object, but you won't get something that is both true square and true circle. Square circles are unconditionally, absolutely impossible. They are logical contradictions that cannot exist. They aren't, therefore, even *things*. In order for something to qualify as a "thing," it must at least be logically possible (i.e., absolutely possible) that it could exist. But square circles don't even meet that condition, so that they aren't things.

All right, now let's return to the omnipotence paradoxes. Can God create a square circle (where the definitions of "square" and "circle" are the same as we understand them)? The answer must be no, because square circles are absolutely impossible. But aren't we limiting God then? Again, the answer is no. Think back to the definition of omnipotence, namely that God can do anything. Well, Lewis asks that we take that seriously, any-*thing*. Square circles aren't things. So, saying that God cannot make them isn't limiting at all, for they are nothing, and nothing cannot be made, can it? In fact, we can go so far as to say that the notion of absolute impossibility, logical impossibility, *defines* (rather than limits) God's power. We now understand much better what we mean when we say that God can do anything.

Notice that God can do all the things that are beyond our wildest imaginings—yes, yes, yes—because these are *things*. He can make blue cabbage and skinny walruses and even moons made out of cheese. But he cannot make non-things, because they aren't possible things. The omnipotence paradoxes talk of non-things as though they were things, and then they demand that God create them ... well, crafty verbiage hardly qualifies as a real objection.

If God cannot create contradictions because there's nothing there to create, then God also cannot create contradictory states of affairs. Such states are still contradictions, still beyond your conception. Example: try to imagine a state of affairs in which a dog both barks and doesn't bark in the same exact way in the same exact time. You can't do it, can you? Because what I gave with one hand, barking, I took away with the other, non-barking. I can't have it both ways.

God cannot make such a dog either, because there's no actual condition being offered for God to create. It's not even a test of his creative power, because creative power creates *things*!

I'll bet you're starting to see the resolution of the omnipotence paradoxes now, aren't you? Isn't God killing himself just such a contradiction? How can God who exists necessarily cancel (render unnecessary) his existence? God is necessary, so he cannot not be. Thus, *to ask that he not be is to ask the one whose essence is to be not to be!* That's a mouthful, so go back and reread that sentence. Or again, how can God create a universe where he omnipotently exists and a rock too heavy for him to lift also exists? Such a universe is itself a contradiction. It's not a possible state of affairs. So, it's not a challenge to God's power at all, because God can do any logically possible state of affairs.

Now, let's ask another question about God's power: how is it compatible with the creation of a free person? If God makes us free, doesn't that action bind him to our decisions? Doesn't his sovereignty and power mean that we must be entirely determined? Well, if we are entirely determined, then God is responsible for evil, and we'll see next chapter how that is impossible (yes, absolutely so). But to address the freedom issue itself, consider that if ever God acts, it is the case that he acted, and he cannot un-act what he acted, or else he didn't act. Thus, God "binds" himself if ever he acts. But this really isn't binding, for the alternative is to say that God is so powerful that he cannot act at all! Hence, to say that God can act means that he commits himself to what he does. So, if he creates a free agent, then he cannot render that freedom void by counteracting all that creature's actions. Otherwise, that being isn't free. God has the choice either to make the being free and then allow it its free choices, or to not make it free at all. He can do either one. He cannot do both, again, on pain of contradiction. God's omnipotent power does *not* demand that he *not* create free creatures. Theism (believing in God's existence) does not require believing in determinism (the denial of freedom).

But we might object that then we could do things against his desires. True. But in creating us as persons (as free agents), he knew that full well. It doesn't undermine his power that we commit evil actions. Rather, his power created our freedom in the first place. His creative choice—a demonstration of his power—means that he cannot overly interfere with our affairs. He can limit our powers, of course. Perhaps you should consider how much more damage we could do to one another if we possessed angelic capabilities like telepathy! But God has to allow us to do evil if we really are free. If every time I try to stab you with a knife it turns to butter, then I just cannot act freely. Lewis says that for God to make free agents (without telepathy) like ourselves there must be a neutral medium between them, what we all call the natural world. The natural world can be counted on to remain pretty much stable, so that we can manipulate it in order to communicate with other minds. We can move our mouths to speak. We can write books and create television programs to convey ideas. But we can thereby also count on it to be stable for evil purposes. Those books might inspire very damaging behavior. This is the consequence of creating free agents.

You might wonder why freedom can be worth it . . . well, just consider how valuable a thing love is. Love is freely chosen. God cannot make us love him, or else it wouldn't be love. A bride in chains at the altar is not being married, but raped. God is not in the business of divine rape. He is the ultimate lover. But that means that where he creates a being capable of reciprocal love, that being must be able to choose otherwise. But now we're talking of divine goodness, aren't we? Let's return to that subject in our next chapter.

CHAPTER TWELVE

THE DIVINE NATURE: GOODNESS

(St. Thomas Aquinas, *Summa Contra Gentiles*, Bk. I, Chs. 37-41; C. S. Lewis, *The Problem of Pain*, Ch. 3)

We left off our last chapter discussing divine love, a possibility stemming from God's capacity to create creatures who depend upon him for their existence, but whose individual choices depend upon themselves. We call such creatures free agents, or, more particularly, "persons." Persons are the subjects of moral action, because they are responsible for their acts.

Our monotheistic traditions (as well as a great many of the pagan traditions) tell us that man is made in the image of the divine. In discussing divine power, we saw that because God is powerful, he is an actor, one who acts, an agent. To be an agent is to be a person. Thus, we are made persons in the likeness or image of God. Our freedom is a unique and divine gift that makes us like unto the divine nature. Because we are persons, we are capable not only of being loved, but of loving back. St. John the Christian theologian said that we love

God because he first loved us, for God is love. Today we want to explore this concept of God's essential goodness, his divine love.

Let's begin with the concept of divine goodness. Notice four distinct claims that we can make about God's relationship to goodness.

1. God is good.
2. God is the highest good (i.e., God is goodness itself).
3. God is the good of every good (i.e., applied to us, this means that God is *our* good, our end, or our purpose.)
4. God is his own good.

You have probably never heard of the last three of these four, though they are critically important for understanding God's goodness and, ultimately, his love. So, we're going to follow St. Thomas Aquinas through his discussion of the meaning and proofs of these claims about God's nature.

Let's begin with the notion that God is good. How do we know that this is true? Mightn't it be possible that the universe is really caused by a bad God, by a cosmic jinni of sorts? Looking around at all of the trouble in this life, you might wonder if that is so farfetched! We'll examine this possibility seriously in a later chapter. By applying a little bit of philosophical reasoning to our understanding of God's nature, we can see that this is in fact impossible. The three "omni" attributes—omnipotence (infinite power), omniscience (infinite knowledge), and omnibenevolence (infinite goodness)—are mutually entailing. This means that if any one of them applies, then they all do. Let's try to understand why this is so.

Let's begin with how omnipotence and omniscience are mutually entailing. If God is all powerful, then he can make himself know everything. Therefore, omnipotence entails omniscience. Similarly, if God is omniscient, then he knows how to do anything—in which case he is omnipotent. This mutual relationship isn't difficult to see. What's harder to understand is why omniscience and omnipotence entail omnibenevolence.

To get at this, we need to think further about goodness. What is it? What makes a father who cares for his son, stays up with him at night when he is throwing up, teaches him how to repair his bicycle tires, goes fishing with him on Saturday mornings, educates him in all areas of human understanding, games with him in computer, table top, and athletic games, teaches him how to drive, supports him through college, advises him wisely in matters of love, and offers him loving support in being the best person that he can be . . . a *good* father? And by contrast, what makes a father who despises his son, poisons him to make him sick and then laughs at him when he throws up, smashes his bicycle with a sledge hammer, mocks him when he fails to catch anything when he went fishing by himself, ridicules him for any intellectual or creative endeavor, decidedly defeats him in all games that they play (and quits playing when his son starts to get good), refuses to let him drive, laughs at him when he says he'd like to go to college and recommends instead he apply to work as a "sanitation engineer," takes him to a strip joint to learn about love, and finally, demands that he enter a life of crime to support the family . . . a *bad* father? Hmm . . . well, mull that one over. What do you think? Isn't what makes a father good or bad entirely dependent on whether he seeks what is good for his son? We are good when we act according to what is good for things. To do that, we need to know what the things are. Thus, to act good toward a rabbit is different than to act good toward a human being. To act good to your son, you need to consider who your son is.

I want you to see the relationship between goodness and being (what a thing is.) Aristotle says that we act well (i.e., good) when we act toward completing the natures of things. Thus, to act well is to act according to what is, according to nature. The good father fulfills his son's human nature, while the bad one undermines it. Goodness is the substance of things, evil its detraction or deprivation. The philosophers call this the "privation theory of evil." Evil isn't substantive or robust. It doesn't have being or nature. Rather, it is the lack of being or nature in something that ought to be different. Evil isn't a positive thing, but the lack of a positive thing.

Evil is like darkness, the absence of light. Evil is like cold, the absence of heat. The real, the robust thing is the good. Evil is a leech that simply eats away at the full nature of a thing. Now, with this in mind let's go back to the question we were asking about God. Is it possible that an omnipotent being could be evil? Well, if a being is omnipotent, then he possesses maximal reality, all positive qualities, doesn't he? And to possess maximal reality means that he is lacking in nothing, including goodness. Since evil is a lack—a privation—it follows that since God lacks nothing, he cannot be evil. So, it is impossible for an infinite being to be evil. Thus, divine omnipotence entails divine goodness.

Now, you might object that maybe the privation theory of evil is false. Maybe evil and goodness are more like yin and yang, two sides of the same ultimate thing. Well, let's consider that. First, you can probably see that this theory doesn't get rid of the privation theory at all, but only fails to call it "evil." For if good and evil are like the choice between cookies or cake, both substantive options, then we can still suggest a third option, namely the negation of both. Thus, privation is back. Second, it's really not clear what could be meant by saying that cookies are good and cake is bad. Both are created things, so how can they be bad in themselves? What can that even *mean*?

Americans were introduced to this idea of good and evil as substances (a doctrine historically called Manichaeism) through the Star Wars trilogy (the original trilogy, that is). In these films it is suggested that good (light) and evil (darkness) are really two sides of the same Force. What the Force is isn't ever very clear. Certain human attributes tend toward the light side of the force, attributes such as calm, self-control, order, and harmony. Certain human attributes tend toward the dark side of the force, attributes such as fear, anger, and excitement. So, as Luke Skywalker learns the ways of Jedi, he is instructed in how to develop one set of human faculties and restrain the other set. He is told that his anger will lead to the seduction of the dark side of the Force, which is what happened to his father. As a result, by the time of the third film, *Return of the Jedi*, we see a very interesting Luke Skywalker. He is neither the boy we met in Star Wars, but nor is he the flamboyant and energetic man that Han Solo is. Instead he is rather odd, calm, and not too passionate. When he faces off against Han's enemies, he fights them rather dispassionately too, always on guard against the emotions that "lead to the dark side." Finally, he faces Vader and the Emperor, and there he is told that he will succumb to the power of the dark side of the Force. The Emperor tries to create a dilemma for Luke: either Luke will be killed by Vader and thus eliminated, or he will defeat Vader by giving in to his passions and thus fall into the dark side of the Force. Either way, the Emperor wins. And so, Luke fights Vader, and starts to lose the battle, but he also refuses to give into the Emperor. Then Vader reads into Luke's mind and realizes that Luke's sister is Leia, and Vader threatens her, "If you will not submit to the power of the dark side, then she might!" And of course, Luke completely loses it, furiously engaging Vader with a series of light saber strokes that bring Vader to his knees in defeat. At this point, according to the Manichean theory of the films, Luke ought to fall into the dark side, for he became afraid for his sister and angry . . . yet, strangely, this does not occur. In fact, you probably never noticed this contradiction in the films, did you? Why? Simple: we all know that when someone threatens your sister, you FIGHT. It's not wrong, but right. Anger was made *for* something, after all. The film's writers know that we all feel this way, and so they could slip in this anti-Manichean idea in order to save Luke. But they cheat, don't they? Anger was supposed to be bad, so how can it now be good?

Well, the answer, of course, is that none of us believe in the Manichean theory. We think instead that all substantive human emotions have a proper object, that none of them are inherently bad like the Star Wars theory suggests. In fact, the Star Wars Jedi is being *reduced* in his human nature—made less human—by cutting off parts of his nature (those of you who have read the Stoics will see an immediate parallel). The true human hero is really Han Solo who is becoming a fully human person, a responsible adult male.

Now, what does all this Star Wars talk have to do with the question? Well, theoretically we saw that Manichaeism (the idea that goodness and evil are both substances) was untenable, because we can just recreate the privational question by negating both substances. But I wanted you to see that practically Manichaeism is just as untenable; we don't buy it. Good things are real things. Evil is the absence of the true good, some perversion or corruption of the whole. It often deceives us into thinking that it is positive (that is its seduction), but in the end it is always destructive.

Example: the prostitute. Why is a prostitute attractive to men? Well, she offers them a positive good—sex—together with short term intimacy, in a way that is completely in their control (they are buying her charms). How on the privation theory of evil can this be an evil? Each positive thing that she offers has been robbed of its fullness. It is as though imitators have stepped forward claiming to be the real things. Sex without intimacy doesn't actually satisfy human beings very well, because human sexuality isn't merely physical, but deeply emotional. This is why you aren't awkward about seeing someone you shook hands with yesterday, but you are very awkward when you again see someone with whom you had a one-night stand. Again, the prostitute claims to offer intimacy; she coos and talks dirty and seems so caring . . . yes, but none of this is *real*, is it? In fact, she doesn't care at all. Ask yourself which is better, a woman who really cares about you and loves you sexually, or a woman who pretends to care about you? Is deception better than reality? The reason why prostitution is bad is precisely that it pretends to be the real thing, when in fact it is a privation of the real thing. Why is it attractive to some men? Because it appears to offer them all the sexual rewards without any of the human relationship work, thus catering to laziness. But it doesn't offer any real good in the end. I hope you can start to see why goodness is the real, the substance, and why evil is the privation, the leech, the absence of goodness.

What follows are some pretty astonishing facts for most Americans to consider, but which the ancients thought were completely obvious. What, you ask? *Happiness is not relative to the individual.* Rather, happiness is the good of the human person, and since human persons are distinct kinds of beings (we're neither rabbits nor angels), it follows that what makes us full persons is definitive and the key to our happiness. What is good for us is real. That's why you can tell that of the two fathers I presented at the beginning of this chapter, one of them is a good father, and one of them is a bad father. The father who tends toward his son's true good, the completeness of his human nature, is the good father.

Let's return to the divine nature, and you'll see some truly stunning things. We now understand why God is good. As infinitely real, infinitely substantive, he cannot lack anything at all, and so he must be good. But he is also *the* good, i.e., goodness itself. God is goodness inherently, because he is the standard of goodness. Why? Because he is that person who is absolute perfection. His goodness is uncreated, while ours is created and participates in his. We are good only to the degree that we participate in his being and creation, i.e., according to what is real—our natures. He is good by his eternal participation with himself. This is why God is also his own good. He is not fulfilled by taking in things from without, since he is already maximally fulfilled. We are not our own good, because our completion depends upon us becoming something that we are not currently. And what is that thing? Well, that brings us to the remaining Thomistic principle, that God is the good of every good, in other words, the supreme good, and therefore, *our* supreme good. All created things are aimed at something else for their perfection, but the most and maximally perfect being of all is God. Therefore, God is our supreme end, the one person alone that brings about complete perfection of our being.

To think of it another way, God is good for us. If he is the good, it follows he must be good for us. The moral law is likewise good for us. If we've never understood it as anything but a list of regulations and rules that gets in the way of our fun, it might be time to rethink why honesty, and love, and friendship, and industry, and contentment, and honor, and fidelity are so much better for us than deceit, and hatred, and enmity, and laziness, and theft, and jealousy, and rebellion, and adultery! The virtues are so much better than the vices, because only through them can we achieve true happiness as persons, as people needing to love and be loved. And God is the ultimate lover, for he is the ultimate good. Thus, loving him must be the greatest thing you could possibly do. Perhaps you can see why when asked what the greatest commandment was, Jesus replied to love God with all of yourself.

Now that we've explored God's goodness, we need to connect his goodness to his love. In our next chapter, we'll explore divine love.

CHAPTER THIRTEEN

THE DIVINE NATURE: LOVE

(C. S. Lewis, *The Problem of Pain*, Ch. 3)

In our last chapter, we looked at God's nature, specifically his goodness, and we noted not only that God is good, but that he is the good of all things (including us), and that he is his own good. God is goodness itself. There is no lack in God of anything. The medieval philosophers said that God is the good, the true, the real, and the beautiful. Perhaps you can see why these maximal qualities coexist in the divine nature.

But God is not just universal ideas, or a set of concepts. According to the traditional philosophical and religious arguments, God is a real person too, an agent capable of doing things. As such, he is good and does good things. This is where God's love comes in, for when we say that God is goodness, we mean in part that he acts toward other things according to their goods, toward the fulfillment of their natures. (We'll deal with the possibility that he fails to do this in a later chapter, when we confront the famous problem of evil, i.e., why God seemingly fails to act according to what is good for us. But before we can deal with philosophical problems about God, we first must understand his nature according to the traditions.)

C. S. Lewis, the famous 20th Century Christian writer, presented an intriguing argument concerning God's love in *The Problem of Pain*. He suggested that we not confuse God's love with our less powerful notion of kindness. What is the difference between kindness and love? Lewis maintained that kindness is a grandfatherly quality that seeks to minimize pain in its object. You can imagine the old couple sitting on the bleachers wincing as the coach releases a verbal tirade against his players! But maybe the players need that scathing in order to get back out onto the court and win the game. Compare again the usual grandparent to the parent. Parents cannot think only of minimizing pain in their children. Good parents realize that sometimes their children need to suffer a little bit in order to learn from their mistakes. Pain is actually an exquisite teacher; it's remarkable how fast a D in a class motivates a student.

Love differs from kindness because love seeks the complete good of its object, not merely its comfort. In fact we often talk about being comfortably complacent, i.e., getting used to living lives that aren't very satisfying. So, at best, kindness is a minimal virtue, but it's nothing compared to the greatness and power of real love.

How does all of this apply to God? Well, we began this chapter reminding ourselves that God is not just good but goodness itself, supremely good. That means he seeks the very best for us and won't settle for less. Sounds more like a coach and less like a grandparent, doesn't he? If we think of God as a senile old gentleman, we'll make serious errors in our predictions of his actions. But if we think of God as the ultimate lover . . . well, that's what we need to understand.

Lewis asks us to think about how loves differ from one another. He notes that the religious tradition describes God's love for us using a variety of different images. Consider the famous image of the potter and the clay. On this model, God is the potter and he shapes the clay to his will. We are the clay, the shaped thing, ultimately being prepared to be fired and set as a work of art. This clearly links up human destiny with beauty, but it's not very personal, because the love is not reciprocal. Clay can't love you back.

The second image Lewis draws from the religious tradition is that of the shepherd and the sheep. On this model, according to the Hebrew Bible, God is the shepherd who cares for and tries to keep the (often stubborn) sheep in line. For the Christians, Jesus is the good shepherd who gives his life to rescue the sheep. Now this model is more interesting than the former one, because at least we are living creatures! But being a divine pet might prove less than appealing to you. Nevertheless, we get a definitive notion of divine care and, on the Christian model, divine sacrifice. But it's still not a very satisfying image, as whatever a sheep feels for its shepherd, we'd probably be reluctant to classify it as love.

For his third image Lewis portrays sonship. On this model, God is our father and we are his children, either by nature, or (for the Christians) through baptism into his family. This image definitely raises the stakes, for at least now we are relating to God as persons. And we are expected on this image to fulfill our natures by becoming like our father, our exemplar. But though this model is a vast improvement in imagery over the thing or the beast, it still treats man as a child needing maturity, needing chastening (of course, this might be true, mightn't it?).

For his final image, Lewis draws on the many religious traditions (including the pagan) that see in sexual love the ultimate model of divine love. Interestingly, it's also our highest model of human love. Marriage denotes a reciprocal, loving, permanent fidelity toward one's partner's highest good. It won't settle for anything less. Sometimes we talk about love "accepting the other person," but we have to be very careful in using this language. We rightly mean that we cannot change the other person's essential personality and qualities. But we mustn't mean that we accept their poor behavior, wrong choices, and otherwise wretched lives. Love seeks the good for its object, so love doesn't tolerate bad behavior; on the contrary, it seeks to motivate change. Take a look at the Hebrew Biblical prophet Hosea and how God uses Hosea's futile love for his prostituting wife as an example of God's unceasing attempts to woo the unfaithful Israelites back to loving fidelity with himself. Or think of the dating relationship, how one always puts the best foot forward, looking nice, talking nice, acting nice . . . why? To offer the impression that you *are* nice. Why does this matter? Because being good to other people matters, especially to the people that you love. Granted, we sometimes act the worst toward and around the people we claim to love, but if we reflected on that behavior, we'd probably realize that to just that extent our claims are vacuous. For how can love seek the harm of its object? No, true love seeks the best good for its object, and this means that God seeks the highest good for us.

Naturally, this might prove worrisome to us. Perhaps the gals have a greater insight here, because they live as the pursued in relationships, hoping to attract the right sort and to be rid of the wrong sort. With respect to God, we are all feminine, for he is the ultimate masculine, the ultimate pursuing lover. There's a funny story in the Hebrew Bible where Moses comes down from that thundering mountain (where he's been talking to God), and he tells the people to prepare themselves, because tomorrow God is going to come down into the camp and meet them. Shaking in terror, they tell Moses, thank you very much, but really, please go back up the mountain and talk to God up there. We all know the sexual nervousness of the virgin bride. How much greater then must be the fear of meeting God face to face?

All right, we've spent a good deal of time talking about God's love for us, but perhaps we should talk about the other side of things, our love for God. If love seeks the good for its object, how can we possibly love God? What good could we do him? This is an excellent question, because we're often told that the love of God is the greatest commandment. Could this be one of those weird theological paradoxes? If so, we must examine it to seek resolution.

Let's begin by considering an interesting and specifically Christian doctrine. We can imagine that the Jews and Muslims would say that God loves his creation. But do they say that God *is* love? It's one thing to say that God loves. It's another thing to say that God is love itself. Consider what it would mean if God were essentially love. Since love is a relation between persons, it would mean that prior to creation, God would have had to have someone to love. But who? The Christians have an intriguing answer to this in their doctrine of the Holy Trinity. They claim that God is actually three persons in one divine substance. Thus, God eternally loves himself through the mutual and reciprocating love of the Father, the Son, and the Holy Spirit. Therefore, he would be love essentially, even if he had never created anything.

Now how does this little foray into Christian theology help us? Well, we were trying to understand what it means for us to love God. And now we have a model for what it means for God to love God. I thought perhaps we could use that idea of divine triune love as an example of how we might love God. So, how do the members of the Holy Trinity love one another? The Christians offer us a unique insight into this relationship, when St. John relates the prayer that Jesus offered to his Father when he was in the Garden of Gethsemane just prior to his passion. You can find this prayer in St. John's gospel, Chapter 17. Take a look at that, and notice in the first five verses how Jesus three times reports that he glorified the Father, doing the work that the Father had given to him, and now he is asking that the Father return to him the glory that he had with him from the beginning. What can we learn from this? Apparently, the central operation between the members of the trinity is what Jesus calls "glorification." The word *doxazo* is the Greek term translated as "glorify." The root word is *doxa* which you might be familiar with from the famous doxology. What does *doxa* mean? It refers to an opinion or idea about something, in this case, God himself. Now God obviously has a true opinion about God, so the *doxa* of God is the true and complete manifestation or appearance of God, and this is why it is translated as "glory," since the glory of a thing is its true nature shining through.

Why is this important? Because Jesus doesn't refer to his love for the Father or the Father's love for him; instead he talks of glory. Why? Think back to what St. Thomas said about God's being his own good, i.e., already possessing within himself completion. God cannot seek a good for himself other than himself, and he's already himself (obviously). All God can do is exult in a good already achieved.

Consider an example: suppose you are about to run a 5K race. I might seek your victory by encouraging you, offering you water, and urging you on near the finish line. But once you get there and win the race, then what will I do? I won't seek that good for you (what would be the point of that?), but instead I'll congratulate you and honor you for a good that you've achieved. In the case of God, there is no seeking a good not achieved. For God it's always honoring and exulting in a good that is eternally achieved. To love God isn't to seek an absent good, but to glory in a present good. Thus, for loving God the operating mode is called *glorification*!

Thus does Jesus glorify the Father, and thus does he seek again the glory he had with the Father prior to the Incarnation. Jesus is talking about the divine love between the members of the trinity. Glorification isn't greater than love; glorification *is* love for God.

So, how then do we love God? The same way Jesus models for us, exulting in a good already achieved and seeking in ourselves to participate in that good by completing our nature, becoming full and loving human beings. Have you ever asked the question, what is religion for? If the greatest commandment really is to love God most of all, then perhaps our chapter today could help us answer that religious question. If a mutual intimate love of God is our supreme good, just as the marital imagery suggests, then our purpose in life is to become fit lovers for God, the most perfect bride possible. Perhaps you can see why the second greatest commandment is that we love one another.

CHAPTER FOURTEEN

THE EXISTENCE OF ANGELS

(Peter Kreeft, *Angels (and Demons)*)

We've been discussing the subject of the divine nature. I wonder if you notice a strange gap between human beings and God. Consider: God is an infinite, incorporeal substance, while we are finite corporeal substances (we have bodies). Do you see what lies between these two kinds of beings? A finite incorporeal substance, i.e., a being who is disembodied by nature (incorporeal)—like God—but created (and thus finite). What can philosophy tell us about these beings? We know that we exist, because we see and experience human nature all the time. We can do philosophical proofs for the existence of God, so philosophy offers us insight into God's existence and nature. But what about the huge gap, an infinite one, between God and us?

First, philosophy can show us that there's nothing incoherent about a pure spirit being, a finite incorporeal mind (for that's what "spirit" means metaphysically). It's as possible as anything else. If God doesn't need a body, he could easily have made some creatures who have no need for bodies either.

Certainly there's nothing about being a mind that necessitates a body! All that's required is that one thinks. Of course, human thinking makes use of a brain. But that's nothing but a feature of *human* experience. We don't want to make the mistake of thinking that how something works for us reveals how it *must* work for all things. God doesn't have a brain, but he can think. So, there might well be beings who, like God, are incorporeal (no bodies or brains) but nevertheless think. So, philosophy shows us that finite incorporeal substances are possible.

Second, the medieval philosophers thought that philosophy could go one step further and show us that finite incorporeal substances are probable. Here's their argument, and I'll let you mull over whether it has some merit or not: When we look at the physical plane of existence, we find that every category of being not only contains some members but is chock full of them. At the bottom of the stack we find inanimate matter (rocks). There are many kinds of objects that fall into this classification. Next up the chain of being (things that exist, i.e.), we find animate beings, starting with plants. There are many kinds of plants. Again, we move up the chain, and we find animals. Again, there are many kinds of animals. "Many" doesn't seem to cut it, does it? It might be better to say that we find overwhelming numbers in a variety of kinds that boggles the imagination! And then up the chain again and we find a special kind of animal possessing thought, namely human beings. There are a lot of us too. And then up the chain and we find a category that is completely empty? Incorporeal substances could exist, but there's nothing there at all? The medieval philosophers thought that unlikely given the way God created everything else in abundance. And so, they concluded that it was likely, or probable, that incorporeal substances exist.

But that's as far as philosophy can go on the subject of whether a particular kind of being exists. At some point, one has to actually meet one in order to know for sure. But that takes us straight into the religious traditions, doesn't it?

FAITH & REFLECTION

Let's start with the Jewish tradition, and we'll use that to illuminate the pagan and Christian traditions. Judaism begins with Abraham living in Sumer (you can read his story if you read Genesis chapters 12 and on), and while he is there, a god speaks to him. This god is from Palestine, and he asks Abraham to come to a new land. Abraham agrees to go, and he gathers up his family and heads toward Palestine. Now, we know that Abraham is not a monotheist (believing in just one supreme deity) yet, because his family brings along all their Sumerian idols! And Abraham doesn't object to this whatsoever.

Once they get to Palestine, Abraham approaches the city of Salem (what would later become Jerusalem), and out comes this fellow named Melchizedek who reports to Abraham that he is the priest of the Most High God. Now this is curious, because Abraham realizes that Melchizedek's god is the one who called him to Palestine. But now we get a really interesting fact about this god: he's the "most high" god. In other words, no other god is higher. But notice that this does not mean that this god is supremely high such that no god could ever be as high. What Melchizedek tells Abraham is consistent with the pagan view of gods like Zeus who are currently the highest but who might have been less in the past and might be less in the future. But at least Abraham realizes that this god isn't just some lesser deity; he's pretty tough stuff.

Now this is as far as we get in the Jewish tradition until we come to Moses. You'll recall the story, I'm sure, when Moses is wandering around the wilderness with his sheep and comes upon a burning bush? You can read about this account in the Hebrew Biblical book of Exodus. From the bush he hears a voice that identifies itself as coming from the god of Abraham! Moses asks who this god is (remember, he grew up in Egypt and knew all about their pantheon of gods: Horus, Isis, Osiris, Amun, the whole lot). What we get in response is one of the greatest mysteries of religious history. This god tells Moses that his name is "I am." You can just imagine Moses wondering, "Huh?"

What kind of name is that? Why not George, or Henry, or Frank, or Matilda? "I am"?

We begin to understand the significance of this name when we realize that for the Hebrew people names aren't arbitrary but reveal the natures of things. So, the god of Abraham is telling Moses that he's not just the Most High. He's telling Moses that he is being itself, the one whose nature it is to exist. That requires omnipotence, for only omnipotence can sustain independent existence. It follows further that such a being is infinite. So, this god just told Moses that he's not just *a* god, but he is *the* God (thus bringing about our current usage of the upper case *G* when referring to him.)

Obviously, Melchizedek was right, for the Supreme Being is indeed most high. Why? Because he is highest in principle. So, God reveals his true identity to Moses, and then launches into a major campaign to reclaim his people from the slavery to the Egyptians. If you remember the story of Exodus, you'll recall that God immediately begins a series of plagues upon the Egyptians. But he tells Moses something very interesting about what he's up to. He says that he intends to acquire glory from the gods of Egypt. God isn't really fighting the Egyptian people but their gods. The implication seems to be that their gods are as real as God himself is. (And recall too that these pagan deities supplied their priests with the power to duplicate the first four plagues!)

Now, how does this account square with the *monotheistic* tradition of just one God? Actually, there's no trouble at all, since the term "god" merely means "a spirit being," i.e., an incorporeal substance. In fact, the Hebrew Bible specifically refers to the pagan deities as gods. In one of the texts of the Chronicles, e.g., the God of Israel even calls a high council of all the gods! And in the Psalms God himself refers to these other beings as gods. So, what the monotheistic tradition does is to identify one such god as being much more than one among many. For this God is supreme, meaning he is the creator of all the others. Thus, he is fundamentally different in kind from the other created beings. What's more, it follows from our discussion of the divine nature in our last few chapters, that God alone is the supreme uncreated good, and therefore, only he is worthy of worship. So, there is a claim to exclusive worship made by the God of the Jews (and later, the Christians and Muslims who continue that monotheistic tradition). But nowhere do these traditions rule out the possibility that other spirit beings exist. In fact, Christianity not only affirms the gods, it makes important use of them! Let's see how.

The Christian story begins (in St. Matthew's gospel or St. Luke's if you don't know the story) with a woman named Mary and an angel named Gabriel who comes down from heaven to inform her that she has been chosen to bear the son of God into the world. Now, *what* is an angel? An angel is a finite incorporeal substance, specifically one who functions as a messenger (the Greek term *angelos* means messenger) from God. The Christians reserve the use of the term "angel" mostly to mean those finite incorporeal substances who have chosen to love and serve God. In contrast, the Christians call those finite incorporeal substances who have chosen to reject the love of God "demons."

But angels and demons are nothing other than the "gods" of the Hebrew Bible! They are all of them finite spirits, minds for whom body is not a part of their nature. You might wonder why the Christian tradition so rigidly divides them up into angels (good) and demons (bad). The answer is two-fold. First, all minds are persons, i.e., agents capable of action. As such, angels and demons are persons capable of good or bad, of love or malice. They are likewise free to choose between good and evil, just as we are. You cannot be a person unless you are free to act, and, thus, free to choose good or evil. Second, whereas human beings make their choice for good or evil throughout the whole of their lives, angels and demons don't inhabit the same kind of time as we do. Their time isn't physical. They aren't maturing to become their full selves. Instead, they were complete in themselves from the moment of their creation. So, when they act, they act with the whole of themselves, altogether for good or for evil.

Thus, they all have already made their fundamental choice. Our choice is being made through time as we develop good or bad habits, what the philosophers call virtues or vices, for our choices take the form of habit. Habits form our character. And our character is who we really are, good or bad. But angels and demons aren't embodied, and, therefore, they don't form habits. They choose once for all, entirely with their whole self. Thus, the Christians call the ancients gods (or spirits) angels or demons, depending on which side they originally chose.

Now that we know that "angel," "demon," "spirit," "god," and "finite incorporeal substance" all refer to the same class of being, we can think further about their nature and existence. Let's start with the latter. Obviously, it's quite popular nowadays to discount angels as being mere figments of the imagination. But popularity doesn't have any impact on the myriad of ancient (and sometimes present) reports of encounters with these kinds of beings. The pagan peoples lived in a world in communion with the spiritual (meaning belief in real spirits, not the California kind of "spirituality"). When the Christians preached their message of Jesus to the world, they didn't encounter opposition from physicalists, people who think that the only things that exist are physical. The ancients had enough sense to realize that something within human nature was itself spiritual, for we too *think*. In fact, Aristotle said that it was this very capacity that made us like God. And the Jews said that man was made in the image of God, i.e., as a spiritual person. Moreover, Socrates, in talking about the immortality of the soul, made the argument that the soul must be something special—something spiritual—so that while the body can fall into decay and death, the soul cannot ever die.

Nevertheless, you might rebut in frustration, they might all be wrong. Maybe Mary and Moses and Socrates and Aristotle and Jesus and all the rest were all of them completely out of their minds, as mad as the Mad Hatter! Possible. So, do we have *any **real*** evidence that these beings exist?

Of course, this is a tough question to answer, because one wonders what will count as "real" for you, if you take this extreme physicalist view of things. But it's not like we're cut off from this spiritual world nowadays. We just give it a different name: the paranormal. Paranormal experiences occur to many, many people in consistent, categorical, and physically inexplicable ways. Take out-of-body experiences (often connected to near-death states), for example, which if you study them you will find it difficult to explain the knowledge these people possess after their experience without considering the possibility they weren't exactly "in" their body during the event. Or again, what about remote viewing, a program that until 1994 was highly classified by our government but which was run as a psychic espionage program? Notice that it wasn't experimental but operational. Or again, what about ghostly encounters or their darker cousins, demonic experience and possession? Are all of these people nuts too? Every one of these kinds of events is what the ancient religious traditions report too, just by different names. All of them point to elements of human experience that are inexplicable without some appeal to beings higher than ourselves and lower than God.

The truth is that we won't know 'til we look. Have you ever looked and seriously examined these possibilities? The unexamined life is not worth living, Socrates told us at the beginning of our inquiry. Or are you going to take Hume's view, dogmatically insisting that the world is just the way you wish it to be, and anyone who disagrees with you must be crazy?

CHAPTER FIFTEEN

THE NATURE OF ANGELS

(Peter Kreeft, *Angels (and Demons)*)

Last chapter we talked about the possibility that angels (or spirits, gods, incorporeal substances) exist. Many people refer to interventions by beings of this kind for otherwise inexplicable experiences. Some of these events may well constitute evidence for the reality of this class of beings, persons who think and act and choose, but for whom body is unnecessary.

That brings us to the second half of the question of the existence and nature of angels, namely their *nature*. What are angels like?

Well, if you consult popular culture, they are either whimsical little winged diapered babies flying around with harps or bows and arrows, or else they are nearly insane horrors that are dark and mystifying and tyrannical (if the many movies with angels in them are the test of the truth). Both of these characterizations of the angelic are our attempt to create beings after our own likeness that we can either control (the cherubs) or resent (the dark angel idea). The reality is quite something else, if you listen closely to the ancient tradition.

For the first thing to consider is that they are *pure* mind. Their job is to think and employ mental power. That means that they are gigantic minds, huge, immensely greater in capacity and knowledge than Einstein. The littlest angel is probably bigger mentally than all human beings put together. In fact, St. Thomas Aquinas goes so far as to assert that knowledge of the physical world is fully known to them. What we struggle to understand about the natural world, the angels know entirely from the top down! (It makes you doubt the claim that human beings are here on earth in order to know things.)

Angels have no physical medium between themselves, like we do. We require the natural world, a constant physical order, to rest between us, or else we'd be unable to communicate with one another, for our entire interaction takes place through our bodies. This is part of the reason that being a ghost (being a human spirit separated from your body) so freaks us out. It's not a natural state for us. Nor are most ghosts happy. Have you ever noticed that? (No, I'm not referring to Caspar here). Separation from our bodies is not fitting for human beings.

But angels are entirely at home in their incorporeal reality. They know and they think, and they communicate to one another telepathically (that's not the best term because angels may not have passions like we do, so that the root term "pathos" might not apply to angels at all, but since we usually use the term "telepathic" to mean the ability to see into or send messages to another person via the mind alone, we will employ it here). It's precisely because angels are so intellectual, that many Gnostic cults (we'll learn more about them in later chapters) have been duped into thinking that human destiny is to ascend beyond the body and become a pure spirit knowing all sorts of secrets. Obviously, we're *not* angels, and so, our destiny is human, not angelic. There's nothing wrong with our bodies. Shedding our bodies damages our nature; it does not complete it. In all the religious traditions, God made us physical. And in the Christian tradition, God became a man by being born of a woman . . . all the biological muck. And it was good—very, very good. Thus, being an angel isn't metaphysically "better" than being human. It's just different.

On the other hand, angels are much "better" than we are on any number of different levels when we consider their *power*. In a way, all human beings are pretty much similar to one another. We are all "human" (our name, the form of our nature), and we are differentiated from each other by our different bodies. But angels lack bodies, so how are they different from one another? They must be different in the very structure of their minds. In other words, while all of us are members of one common human species, every single angel is a species unto himself! Each angel is as different from the next one as cats and bats and jellyfish are different from one another. The religious tradition echoes this notion too, for when St. John describes his vision of the throne of God he saw the seraphim, the greatest of all the angels. He describes them the way the Hebrew prophet Isaiah described them in his similar vision, namely as beings possessing six wings, completely on fire, flying around the throne of God calling out forever and ever that God is holy, holy, holy. Now, given just this description, you might think that these seraphim are all alike. But St. John adds to the description by (bizarrely) noting that one of the seraphs was all covered in eyes, while another one had the head of a lion and the body of a goat (or something similar). The point is that each of the four that he saw was completely different from the other ones. So, the term "seraph" ("seraphim" is the Hebrew plural) is a functional term (i.e., describes what these angels do), rather than a species term (i.e., naming their nature).

What follows from this Kreeft describes pretty well, namely, the idea that angels exist in a pure hierarchy of power, not remotely democratic, for there is no equality in the angelic ranks. Those ranks are then described as being highest, lowest, and (obviously) middle. And in each of these categories there is itself a distinction of highest, lowest, and middle, giving us the traditional 9 choirs (or ranks) of angels. (Yes, you could keep repeating the principle and generate more and more classifications, until you eventually just got back to the myriad of individual angelic species). But the real point here is that the angels are extremely powerful beings, capable of displays of power on our physical plane (if they chose or were permitted to do so) that could crush human regimes.

The funny thing is that we've been contemplating extra-terrestrial invasion in our science fiction for years. But according to the religious traditions, the invasion already happened. Only it wasn't extra-terrestrial, but extra-cosmic, since angels and demons aren't physical at all, but come from a pure spiritual (i.e., incorporeal) plane of existence.

Obviously, we don't see angels (or demons) sitting on thrones dominating human beings according to the modes of earthly tyrannies! So, what are these beings up to? Well, philosophically, there's not much that we can say to this point. But the religious traditions give us some clues that we can then expand on using our philosophical tools. Since angels are fundamentally minds, their "weapons" are mental, i.e., are *ideas* and ideology. Good angels are eager for people to be good, think well, and do good things, ultimately knowing and loving God. Bad angels, the demons, are eager for the exact opposite. In other words, angels and demons are most concerned with us *morally*.

And this is just what the religious traditions describe with the comical notion of a good little angel sitting on one shoulder and a bad little demon sitting on the other whispering and suggesting things to us. They are not little, of course. But the idea that these beings are mixed up with temptation and its resistance makes sense given the sorts of creatures that they are.

Now, you might wonder why they don't just dominate us and make us all slaves like the science fiction stories so often portray invaders doing to us. But here you have to think very hard about human nature. We are persons just like the angels and demons. That means that we are free agents; our choice for good or evil cannot be forced (or else it isn't real). The good angels respect our freedom the same way that God does. God wants free lovers, not forced slaves. There is no divine rape. But even the demons have to concede this point (for the most part, demonic possession being some kind of exception), since for them to undermine the divine plan of divine love for human beings, they have to motivate us to choose (freely) against God. Mass enslavement wouldn't do at all. And so the conflict is moral. In both the philosophical and religious traditions, the most important question you will ever confront in your life is the choice between good and evil.

Now, you might wonder why the religious tradition describes the demons as being so directed against God's plan for loving human beings. There are different versions of the story, so let me just describe one of them, mixing some of the Jewish and Christian elements. In effect, the angels were created by God and then presented with an astonishing plan that God had devised. He explained that in addition to creating them in their spiritual splendor and glory, and in addition to creating the physical universe that they saw beneath them, he intended to create a mixed being, almost a spiritual/physical amphibian (to borrow from Lewis for a moment): Man. This led to two reactions. Some of the angels reveled in and gloried in the astonishing creativity of God. But some of the others found the novelty of physical/spiritual hybrid beings as rather gross, undignified, and an impure mixing of the "races." (Now I'll add the Christian tradition to the story.) The situation got worse when God next revealed that he planned to create this special kind of creature in order to incarnate himself as one of them, so that he could speak to them face to face. For the dubious angels, this was the last straw. God mixing himself in with such biological muck? He'd clearly lost his senses. And so, their leader, one Lucifer, announced that he was going to take the place of the Most High. Thus came about the rebellion of 1/3 of the angels, their defeat at the hands of Michael (whose name means "Who is like unto God?" Remember, names *mean* things), the fall into earth and casting into hell of the dark angels, and their new status as demons. And their plans in the universe? To thwart the divine plan to create creatures possessing both physical and spiritual traits who would freely love God. How to do that? Moral assault. Show God that his plan was stupid, that even these silly human things will hate God given the chance. And so, they tempt us to reject our nature, reject our supreme good (God himself), and live according to evil.

Philosophically, there's nothing inconsistent about this account. It could well be true. We know it only if the religious tradition actually is in touch with the other side, for there's no way an account of a council of the gods in which the Most High reveals his plans to his angels would ever get to us unless someone who was there told us.

Let's address one or two last little things about angels that you might be wondering about. Why, if angels don't have bodies, are they always represented with man-like bodies, very bright clothes, and wings? Fair question. You probably realize that the wing represents a being of the air, and the angels' realm is the heavens above the earth, so this is fitting. Moreover, when angels appear to human beings, they may well employ wings, to make clear who they are! There are winged beings like the Biblical angel throughout the ancient world. You'll find them in the marble of the Roman forum to this day, as well as in Etruscan coffin art, as well as in Persian reliefs. But just because an angel shows himself with a body and wings, it doesn't follow he is *essentially* an embodied winged creature. If an angel intended to communicate with you, he'd have to do so physically, because you are human and require a natural physical medium for communication. If he talked directly to your mind telepathically, you'd not be able to tell whether these weren't just your own thoughts! So, the religious traditions tell us that angels manifest themselves in human-like bodies, really extremely elaborate "suits," since they aren't real bodies in the sense that we understand them. Angels don't have a passive sensory system, because they don't gain information from sensation like we do. So, an angelic body wouldn't communicate information to the angel. He'd just know directly what was going on around him, rather than through his body. Hence, it's not a "real" body (bi-directionally interactive) as we understand it.

You might wonder too if angels have sex. Kreeft addressed this one, and you can see why, namely because we are very interested in sex! In one sense, of course, they don't have sex, because they don't reproduce, and sexuality is a mode of biological reproduction. Or is it?

The reason I ask this question is because of the way in which the masculine and feminine have been represented throughout the centuries in objects that are non-biological. Take words, for example; in many languages there are masculine and feminine forms of words. Or, again, take the Renaissance paintings of the Virtues (the middle class of the angelic ranks, each Virtue-Angel thinking and developing in others its namesake). All of them are feminine! There's Justice, holding *her* scales. And Charity, and Fortitude, and all the rest. So, the idea here is that the masculine and feminine are larger categories than the male and female that we experience in animal biology. Our experience of these categories is but an imperfect representation of something that may well go all the way up the chain of being. If so, then angels have sex in the same formal way that we do, in that they might well have gender. But the purpose of gender would go way beyond reproduction. What is that purpose? I don't know for sure, but I suspect it has much to do with the nature of love. (We'll talk more about this when we look at *A Severe Mercy*.)

But I will suggest one thing for you to consider. Have you ever noticed how in the Lord's Prayer, Jesus calls God "Father"? Some people think that this is merely cultural prejudice, and that he might just as easily have called on the Mother Goddess. But such thinking is rather new. The ancient tradition tells us that the divine Fatherhood means something important, that in reflecting on our relationship to God, we are all children. Or, again, we call God a divine lover, yes, but the bride? Hardly. God is the divine suitor, the one who seeks out and pursues. Thus, the masculine again. It's become commonplace in the last fifty years to say that gender is nothing but cultural or social construct, and, thus, that we can refer to the divine nature however we want. We can have priests and priestesses in the church. The Ancient Churches of the West and the East (Catholic and Orthodox) disagree, don't they, just as they have for 2,000 years. Why? Well, they are under the impression that God revealed himself to us in natural modes that *he* made. After all, what society or culture existed without husbands and wives, mothers and fathers—male and female? Doesn't gender exist prior to society? Doesn't biology come first? And if God chose to take a masculine form in entering the world and chose to call us his bride, isn't that his prerogative? We may ultimately choose to reject the suitor, but first let's be clear about who we are rejecting.

Finally, consider that all along we enlightened contemporary people might have had it backwards. Maybe we aren't projecting our own social categories onto the divine nature! What if God created us according to his own nature? Isn't that exactly what the Jewish tradition tells us, in that God created man in his own image? Or, again, is God Father because we've foisted human fatherhood onto the heavens, or because God is eternally Father to his eternal Son? On this Christian Trinitarian view, we are privileged to participate biologically in an eternal relationship amongst the members of the godhead.

PART TWO

CHAPTER SIXTEEN

THE SHINING BARRIER

(Sheldon Vanauken, *A Severe Mercy*, Chapters 1-3)

When we think about the intersection of thought & belief, between philosophical reflection and religious life, we realize the enormous contribution philosophy can make to thinking about the ideas in religion. We've looked at faith and reason, miracles and natural law, the existence and nature of God, and the existence and nature of the incorporeal substances. But, throughout our discussion, we've seen some of the limits of conceptual examination. Of course, Socrates didn't tell us that the unexamined *concept* wasn't worth living, did he? He spoke of an unexamined *life* and contrasted it with an examined *life*. So, philosophy for Socrates wasn't a set of ideas so much as a kind of life. In fact, if you think about the etymology of "philosophy" you get two root words—*philo* and *Sophia*. We're familiar with the first term from Philadelphia, the city of brotherly love. Philo is the love of friendship. Sophia is the goddess of wisdom, or just Wisdom. So, a philosopher is a lover of wisdom. Notice philosophy is not an academic discipline. Nor is it one of the "ologies" like geology, the study of something. No, even though there are academic and studious elements to philosophy, it begins and ends as a love, a reciprocal love (like friendship) with Wisdom herself.

Now, if you are a religious person, you'll probably feel something familiar in the way Socrates talks about Wisdom, almost like God. And you're not far from the mark, since Wisdom on the Christian view is the second person of the Trinity, the Wisdom of God, the Eternal Word. In fact, the early Christians quickly found a kindred spirit in Socrates, and St. Justin Martyr wrote a couple of *Apologia* defending the faith to the Emperors of Rome, showing them how Christianity fulfilled all the best aspirations not only of Judaism, but also of pagan philosophy and religion.

When we think about religion, we naturally think about concepts of God and faith and love and law, etc., but we also think about particular kinds of experience, say of the liturgy or prayer or temptation or loss or hardship in life. In other words, religion isn't just theory, is it? It's a kind of life, a life shared with others in community, devoted to certain specific ends, and aimed at a lived love for God. In fact, religion can easily lay claim to its being a lived experience, far more so than philosophy. Most people don't think of philosophy as a kind of life at all, but just deep (or silly!) thinking. But religion affects us from the moment of our birth through all of the most significant events in our lives. Think about how we mark children at birth through circumcision in the Jewish faith, through baptism for the Christians, how we mark their growth and maturity, how we celebrate the marriages in full religious ceremonial pomp, and how ultimately we mourn and commemorate their deaths. At every important stage of life, as well as the daily grind, faith seems essential for many people to find or lay claim to significance.

I want us to think about the intersection of philosophy and religion not just conceptually, then, but also from within lived and shared experience. To do that, we're going to look at three books that are really narratives, stories, of people's experiences with these questions. The first story is called *A Severe*

Mercy. This is a book about people on the outside of faith, who want nothing to do with it, because they love beauty, truth, and goodness. But you can probably guess from what we've described about the nature of God, what ultimately happens to them! In the second story, entitled *Christ the Tiger*, Thomas Howard describes a life from the inside of religion, only he seeks desperately to escape. Why? Because he cannot see how his form of faith can confront the realities that human beings face in their lives.

Now, I should think that most of you can appreciate one or the other of these perspectives, either being on the outside and really not being too thrilled with being drawn in, or being on the inside and discovering an alluring pull away from its promised security and safety. Both narratives will drive us deeply into human experience and the confrontation with faith. What is faith for? How can it possibly work? What on earth is God doing to/with us?

You'll probably note that I mentioned three books. The third book is also a narrative, but it's fiction. Moreover, it's completely pagan. Lest that unnerve you, its author is the celebrated author C. S. Lewis, and it's entitled *Till We Have Faces*. This book is recognized as his greatest literary work ever, even though most people are less familiar with it. I'll not try to tell you what it's about at this point. A fine red wine needs to breathe before it is drunk, and our minds need to percolate on what Vanauken and Howard have to teach us before we can peer into the depths of what Lewis will offer us.

Let's begin then with *A Severe Mercy*. And we'll start with a question: what makes a great love? List for yourself the top seven qualities that make for an enduring intimate love. You'll see that our two characters, Davy and Sheldon, are devoted to such a love. In fact, they commit their lives not only to one another, but toward their love. I'd like you to think specifically about the principles that they employ and compare them to what makes for love these days.

First, notice what they are committing themselves to, an *enduring* love, understood in terms of what they ultimately describe as eternal moments, like the night of sea fire. They understand their love as participating in a life devoted to the beautiful. And in the longing for the beautiful they find the shared substance of their inloveness. Theirs is a notion of consecration, something high and holy, but to their minds entirely pagan. Think about what that means.

In their poem "The Shining Barrier," they present their theory of love and its permanence, namely a thousand strands of sharing, so strong that nothing could ever break it. If something is good enough to be valued by one of them, then they are convinced there must be something in it worth looking at. So, rather than divide their lives, they determine to unite them as fully as they can, allowing none of the usual distractions to draw them away from this intense other-knowledge. For example, they notice how many relationships around them are corrupted by material possessions with arguments about who put the ding in the car! So, they jointly take a hammer and whack their brand new car together, ensuring that that won't be a problem in the future. Children so often separate men and women into particular kinds of unshared or unshareable experience, so they decide that for them, children are out. Furthermore, they reject any secrets at all, since their love depends on total trust. Their decisions must be made jointly, no bosses or "laying down the law." Furthermore, they create what they call the principle of the affirmative, meaning that if one of them believes something and the other person is indifferent to the issue, the other party will choose to believe it too.

They look around in the world and focus on what wrecks once-great loves. They find a lack of decency and courtesy in the world, and aim to center their relationship on the purest courtesy, symbolized for them by the request for a glass of water in the night. It's the courtesy of the requester to offer the other person the opportunity to get up and lovingly provide the water. Just imagine being able to think, feel, and act in that way! What kind of love, kind of trust, kind of non-manipulative and non-deceptive relationship you'd have to have! Additionally, they endorse a principle of spontaneity, to never resist a sudden impulse by either of them, in order to enable creativity in the appreciation of new experience (no ruts for these two).

Why such (what to us might seem) extreme measures in love? Because when they look around them, they see so few older people truly in love. They come to believe that love itself is under assault, attacked by a lack of decency, a loss of courtesy, the mockery of fidelity, and self-regard. They determine that only by the greatest effort can the love, so fragile in its beginnings, have a chance to mature. And so they erect their "shining barrier" to safeguard their love and to prevent the "creeping separateness" that turns once intimate couples into lonely people when they are together. The Shining Barrier will stand, they think, so long as they "build their altar to love." Notice the religious imagery again, the level of consecration necessary to sustain a truly beautiful love.

The Shining Barrier has a meta-level function to it that enables them to stop whatever they are doing, even a fight or problem, in order to rise above it all and remember and recall who they are and how all things must be decided relative to the question of how it will impact their love. They create their "Navigator's Councils" to annually review their love, to see how they are doing, what they can improve. Imagine doing that on your anniversary instead of merely giving flowers or a card! Don't you think it's a bit strange that on this most important aspect of our lives, we spend so little time evaluating how we are actually doing, short of busting out into fights or finally sitting in front of a shrink trying to talk about the things that we might have learned to talk through together from the beginning? (If you're not married, you might ask yourself whether your reflections on love are not wholly the product of popular culture ... what does a fifteen-year-old screaming into a microphone know about real love?)

The final meta-level measure they create is their Appeal to Love, the highest and most powerful appeal that either of them can make to the other one. No matter what the issue is where they are struggling together or with one another, if either of them makes the Appeal to Love, it all stops on the spot, for no matter is so great that it can be permitted to tear down their love.

They worry, as do most couples, about the horror of separation in death, and here too, they develop a plan to prevent this horror from overtaking them. Two people devoted to this level of intimate knowledge of another person could not easily survive sanely without the other person. As such, they plan the Long Last Dive should one of them contract a terminal illness, a concept that shifts to their sinking the Grey Goose under themselves while they sleep, so that even in death, they will go hand in hand, no "sundering of the grip."

What do you think about this relationship? Where are they right? Where are they wrong? Mull that over carefully.

Now, in chapter 3, Vanauken explains what he means by their "high paganism." They believe in and worship Beauty. Do they think it is divine? Yes, they think that something divine must have caused everything, but they don't think of it in terms of goodness, only of beauty. They thought that beauty was the inner meaning and value of all things. Love was an "aspect of beauty." Their lives, therefore, had a religious feel to them in the sense that they really worshipped beauty, Aphrodite, the goddess who captured the beautiful. Vanauken remarks on page 60, "Many an ancient philosopher, and even more, many a Hellenic lyric poet would have approved, or at least sympathized with, our dedication to love and beauty, our trust in reason, and our goal of the good life."

Theirs is a life focused on experiencing all the beauty that can be "teased from time," a life focused on the positive elements. But do you think that's enough? Did they? I'm thinking of the first really dark event that occurs in chapter 3. Take a look at the incident in the park (pg. 67), how it affected Davy, and what her response was. Oddly enough, though she was the victim in the park, the darkness of that incident and her bare escape brought into her mind her own darkness. She becomes aware of her own sin, not only the wrongful acts she committed, but even the "unattempted loveliness," the "costly valour never won," what theologians call sins of omission. Sheldon doesn't really understand what she's experiencing, convinced as he is that she is most definitely *not* a sinner, but his confidence cannot shake her own conviction.

What I'd like you to think about first is the difference between talk of wrongful actions and describing those actions as "sins." What is a sin, anyway? Moralists don't talk that way. You only find that language in religious contexts. Why? It's an important question and I'd like you to think about it carefully. It's one thing to violate a moral standard. It's quite another to violate a person.

Secondly, few people consider religion all that seriously when things are "going well." At least that's what you hear! But when children fall ill, when people lose work, when your sons are called up for military service, when death takes your beloved or crime your sense of security and decency, then you go in search of someone who represents God. Why? What is it about us that shows itself in such deep need (as Davy reveals) for remission and redemption? Nowadays, if we're not religious, we try to chalk these feelings up to various forms of psychological failings, but the ancients wouldn't have been so quick to disregard them. They, like the Jews and the Christians, all saw forgiveness, repentance, reconciliation, and sacrifice as inextricably tied together.

Here's a clue to start you thinking . . . if God isn't just an idea, but a real person, then maybe our moral failings go much deeper than we think, as affronts to deity and its regal claims on our lives. Living in a republic, we rarely think about let alone feel majesty or royalty. But the Vanaukens inhabit a different world in their imagination, a world of valor and nobility, where chivalry and high courtesy have place. But where a world of splendor exists, so does its negation in despair and horror. By flattening the world politically, we might have gone too far and tried to flatten out all that is. But as we saw from our discussion on the angels, theirs is a world of pure hierarchy. In that world, one approaches God on bended knee.

CHAPTER SEVENTEEN

ENCOUNTER WITH LIGHT

(Sheldon Vanauken, *A Severe Mercy*, Ch. 4)

A great many citizens of the United States describe themselves, at least nominally (i.e., in name, if not in practice) as "Christians." Perhaps you are one of them. If not, then you probably are so familiar with that faith that you have strong reasons for rejecting or disliking the name. We are immersed in a world dominated by the aftereffects of a potent Puritan culture.

Why does this matter? Because the experience the Vanaukens describe in their feelings about Christians might be something you have yourself thought about or at least felt! Let me put the question as bluntly as possible: why do people hate Christians? And if "hate" is too strong a term, then reduce it to whatever works for you: "dislike," "feel uncomfortable with," "just plain wish they would bother somebody else," etc. What is it with Christians? And even if you are Christian, I'll bet you've run into people who classify themselves this way for whom you cared very little. You might have been rubbed the wrong way too. Why? We need to understand this reaction that is all too common, because it very much informs the Vanaukens' experience in Virginia. And we need to understand that experience in order to appreciate just how different their experience in Oxford turned out to be.

I hope you've had time to answer that question. If not, before reading on, stop and jot down the top ten reasons people hate Christians! Should be fun.

[Jeopardy Music]

[More Jeopardy Music]

[Still More Jeopardy Music]

Okay, all done? Got your list?

Let's see what's on it . . .

They think they know everything

They are holier than thou, meaning they think that they are better than I am

They have lists of rules that they impose on everybody else

They are hypocrites, condemning others and doing the same or worse things themselves

They talk funny, in their own religious dialect and disdain those who don't get it

They create a religious subculture that isn't all that different from popular culture

They treat non-Christians rather badly

They treat non-Christians very well, so long as their conversion potential remains

They really don't like the world around them very much (so why don't they just *leave?*)

They try to scare people into believing in God on the pain of hell

Does this list strike a familiar chord with you? Regardless of how accurate these impressions are, they are the often-reported impressions people form of self-identifying Christians. And these are the impressions that the Vanaukens had too, only taken up in the imagery and language that they used to describe their experience: Christians are dull, unintelligent, and ugly. Mull over why people have these impressions of Christians.

But on the trip across the ocean, they had a strange experience. Do you recall it? They took up a collection to help the woman who'd lost her money, and as they did so, they encountered many queries as to whether they were *Christians*. Now, this suggests a rather different image of Christians, doesn't it? In this case, the thought was that taking care of another person was something a Christian would be expected to do. The Vanaukens merely thought that it was the sort of thing any decent person would do. But they never really had expected a convergence between Christian faith and decency (of the sort that merged with beauty).

Once they arrived in England they formed a circle of friends at Oxford and discovered that the vast majority of them turned out to be Christians. It wasn't that everyone at Oxford was a Christian. No, on the contrary, many were not. Rather, the sorts of people that Davy and Sheldon *liked* were Christians. This result surprised and bothered them. It surprised them, because they had never thought that anyone could be highly intelligent, civilized, witty, fun to be with, and Christian. It bothered them, because they'd already agreed that Christianity was nothing more than a local superstition. It lacked the universality required of any true worldwide religion, and it just couldn't really be true. People rising from the dead? Come on. But then so many of their friends actually believed these things. Could they be right? Could it be true? Hmm . . . maybe they'd have to have a look.

Before joining them in their examination of the Christian faith, let's try to understand how the Christians they met at Oxford could be so unlike the people they'd known in Virginia. How is it possible that Christianity and Beauty can converge? Didn't our Puritan ancestors teach us that to be a Christian means to abstain from color in clothes, not to enjoy the theatre, reject fun in the name of solemnity, avoid strong or even weak drink for that matter, condemn anyone who plays cards or smokes tobacco, maintain the highest moral standards of dress so as to avoid giving anyone the impression that sex might be fun . . .

Hmm . . . this sounds exactly like what the Vanaukens rejected in Virginia. Those Virginian people lived very much according to this old Puritan code, thinking in effect that to be a Christian meant to withdraw from the world around them. After all, to be a Christian means that you love God instead of the world, and you want to be with him in heaven after you die, and heaven is a place without bodies, so obviously, bodily pleasures must be abandoned to purify the soul and ready it for God!

If that's what Christianity is, then Jesus got it very badly wrong, didn't he? Do you remember what his first miracle was? His mother took him to a wedding and when the host ran out of wine, his mother asked him to do something about it. So, he turned six huge stone pots full of water into pots full of the best wine the steward had ever tasted. He even remarked that no one in his right mind would serve such good stuff now, since the wedding guests were already well past sobriety! But they served it, and Jesus was the one who made the stuff.

Nothing about this picture accords with the Puritan imagery, does it? In fact, the Puritans sound a lot more like Jesus' arch-opponents, the Pharisees, people who created a whole set of rules to safeguard people from ever having to be truly good. And the result? They disdained everyone around them who failed to live up to their code. But the code was arbitrary and had nothing to do with genuine love. So, Jesus took every opportunity he could to screw up their law in order to show them what real love was. In fact, the Gospels record that Jesus had a reputation for hanging out at bars with tax collectors and prostitutes. Why? Because he sought to become greedy and lustful himself? No, not at all. Because those who know they are sick can make use of a physician. The Pharisees' legal codes offered them the false impression that they were perfectly holy, perfectly well. Thus, they didn't find Jesus necessary. T. S. Eliot famously offered the line in one of his poems about people who create systems of morality so perfect that no one will ever have to be good. The Pharisee and the Puritan fit the bill don't they? By setting up rules that say, for example, that wine is bad in itself, no one will ever have to learn the true virtue of self-control (called moderation) with its inherent risk. By just denouncing all gambling as bad in itself, no one ever has to experience the rush that comes from gaming and learn how to control it. You see the how different the law code morality is from real virtue?

What explains the difference in the two views? Well, it all comes down to what religion is *for*. If you think that religion is about going to heaven, and heaven is a place of pure spirit (no bodies), then you might think that the purpose of religion is to turn you into a pure soul. This is a rather popular view of religion's purpose in American right now. But this view runs into real problems when you compare it to the actual Christian tradition in which God is born physically into a body, dies and is resurrected physically, ascends into heaven in a body, and promises to return in a body. And why does he do all this? Not to take the people away to heaven! On the contrary, according to the ancient texts, the idea is that God will destroy the old heavens and earth and recreate a new earth on which his city will descend and in which he will live with his people as a physical person. In other words, the ancient Christian view of religion's purpose is this: to make you perfectly *human*. When God makes the saint, he does not unmake the man. Grace never contradicts nature; it always perfects it.

The Pharisee and the Puritan are two examples of a contrary philosophy best known by its ancient title, Gnosticism. The Gnostic aspires toward angelic spirituality or spiritism. His objective is to ascend away from his body and live on a "higher" plane. As such, he rejects the world around him and pursues a morality of separation from physical things.

But the earliest Christians denounced Gnosticism, St. Paul writing his Colossian letter explicitly to confront their views. He writes that Christians ought not to worship angels (pure spirits) thinking that that is their destiny. Nor should they create elaborate rule codes like the Pharisees did, for these do nothing to enable true virtuous self-control. Instead of rejecting the physical world around them, they should realize that all that God made, both physical and spiritual, is good. And for a being who is both physical and spiritual, which is what human beings are, their final purpose must satisfy *both*.

So, all that is in the world exists for our enjoyment and should be received with thanksgiving, St. Paul writes. But the Christian is not to be controlled by anything (addiction), nor is he to misuse physical things in ways that undermine love for others. In other words, Christians are supposed to mirror the love that Jesus showed people, living fully human, virtuous lives.

The reason why the Vanaukens hated Virginian Christianity is that it wasn't Christianity at all, but its false cousin Gnosticism. Gnostics hate being human. They are like the Little Mermaid, determined that their happiness lies in being someone else. But Christianity so endorses human nature that God became one of us in the incarnation! Once the Vanaukens met real Christians in Oxford, people who loved the world that God made, people who sought beauty, and truth, and goodness, and joy . . . they realized that Christians loved the same things they did. And, thus, were born all their friendships.

They had expected Christianity to present a drab view of the world, when, in fact, the reality was completely the opposite. Puritan New England isn't the hallmark of Christian culture, but Gnostic culture. That's why American is so schizophrenic about Christian faith, as it's been so infected by Gnosticism. No, the true hallmark of Christian culture was the Renaissance, when all the ideas of the medieval philosophers finally bubbled up into a stable cultural setting and blossomed into the intellectual pursuits of Leonardo da Vinci, the sculpture of Michelangelo and Bernini, the painting of Raphael, and the magnificent architectural achievements in cities such as Florence, Pisa, Milan, Venice, and Rome.

It was this fully human, civilizing faith that the Vanaukens first encountered at Oxford, and it's understandable, I think, why they found a continuity between it and the aspirations of the Shining Barrier. But of course, not all that lies within the Shining Barrier proved perfectly compatible with Christianity. In our next chapter, we'll look at the conflict that began to emerge, as the Vanaukens drew closer to faith.

CHAPTER EIGHTEEN

GOD & THE SHINING BARRIER

(Sheldon Vanauken, *A Severe Mercy*, Ch. 5)

In our last chapter, we tried to understand the radical differences in culture, aspiration, and sentiment between the Gnostic religious experience the Vanaukens rejected in Virginia and the historic Christian experience they encountered at Oxford. We can appreciate much better now how their view of love as the longing for the beautiful connected so directly with a view of God who is the good, the true, and the beautiful, who is Love itself.

You might have been surprised at how much the question of the historical truth of Christianity mattered to the Vanaukens. It mattered critically to them, because the claim of Christianity wasn't that it was just another myth, though it has profound mythic force, but that its mythic power lies directly in its claim that the myth became fact. Thus, there *is* a question of fact, a question of truth.

You might compare the Vanaukens' experience of examination and inquiry about the truth of Christianity with the theoretical discussion we had at the outset of this book, reading St. Thomas and Locke on faith and its relationship to reason. None of them take the Gnostic bifurcated view of separating faith from reason, religion from real experience. On the contrary, they all see life as one seamless whole. Thus, the truth of the claims of faith matter a great deal.

But in Sheldon's conversion experience, he seems unsettled by the probability of Christianity's being true. And he seems eager for certainty, and says as much to Lewis in one of his letters. It's worthwhile wondering why certainty cannot, nay, even stronger, shouldn't be had. For the love of God cannot be forced on someone, either in their intellect or in their will. There must be enough evidence to warrant belief, but there must also be enough intellectual room to reject God. For the "faith" of Christianity isn't mere belief, is it? The greatest commandment isn't to believe, but to love. Granted, you cannot love God if you don't believe that he is, but mere belief doesn't transform one into a lover of God or neighbor either.

As the Vanaukens studied the question of whether Christianity was actually true, they also grew to appreciate how their rejection of materialism linked up with Christian metaphysics. They were already convinced that the longing for beauty couldn't be a massive cheat. But in what kind of universe can that longing actually find full consummation? Religious faith offered them an answer that they found extremely compelling.

But religious faith isn't simply a conversion of the intellect to a new belief, though Vanauken insists that it cannot be less. It's the conversion of the entirety of a person, something that Davy felt perhaps more deeply than Sheldon. Think carefully about the intellectual way in which Sheldon approached the question of faith, and the emotional and personal way in which Davy did. Do you think something was lacking in Sheldon's experience? What did Davy's experience add?

We might approach an answer to these questions by reminding ourselves of what drew Davy to God. She was drawn by beauty and truth, just as her husband was. But for Davy, there was something more, wasn't there?

Something portrayed in her sin picture of years past. Davy felt the need for absolution, for reconciliation to God through redemption. You might say that Davy *needed* God. This is part of the reason why she made a decision for Christian faith before her husband, technically in violation of the Shining Barrier.

Sheldon's faith differed from Davy's not just in that his was less animated from emotional need, but also in that his was much more positive in its aspiration. Sheldon almost appears proud in his humility. He views faith as swearing fealty, allegiance to a king, and he almost seems to think that perhaps God ought to appreciate it.

Now, clearly if God is a king, then love for God involves regal recognition of him, so that fealty is not without its value. But we're all familiar with the notion that one doesn't stand in one's approach to God! St. Bonaventure, when asked what were the first four virtues, answered, "Humility, humility, humility, and humility." The Beatitudes begin with poverty of spirit, the recognition of a lack within oneself. This difference between Davy and Sheldon will prove to be quite important as their lives as Christians progress.

Let's turn now to the impact of their Christian conversions on their pagan views, especially those regarding the Shining Barrier. On the one hand, they conclude that what they had been longing for in their desire to get away together on the Grey Goose was the desire for eternal joy. And that joy they now realized could be completed only in God. To that degree, they found deep compatibility with Christianity. But they also wondered whether it would be entirely fitting to just set sail and head off into the sunset in Grey Goose. And they surely realized that at least part of the Shining Barrier had been breached. For now things had to be judged not just from the stand point of "us." "God and us" at least had to be considered. And then there was the Church, and their neighbors, and Christianity even recommends one's attention toward one's enemies! Finally, their suicide pact was completely rejected now that God entered the picture. There could be no long last dive, for life now involved more than just their intimacy. It is true, perhaps, that love offers extraordinary goods for the lovers; but is marriage solely for the sake of the partners? Or does it have benefits and goods that lie outside their union? What is marriage really *for*? Davy and Sheldon had already opened their home, the Studio, to many, many people, so much so that Sheldon chafed a bit for the solitary days aboard Grey Goose. But could they really go back now that they had come so far?

CHAPTER NINETEEN

THE BARRIER BREACHED

(Sheldon Vanauken, *A Severe Mercy*, Ch. 6)

The Vanaukens returned to Virginia from Oxford and immediately felt extreme culture shock. The high civilized lifestyle to which they'd become accustomed was nowhere present in Virginia. But they encountered something else too, a kind of surreal religious experience. In Virginia they found widespread claims to Christian faith, but with none of the shocked reality of it all that they'd encountered at Oxford. They were left aghast, incredulous at what they termed "semi-Christianity." What did this term mean? They felt that the historic, apostolic, and monarchial faith they'd encountered at Oxford was reduced to a mere social and civil experience. Niceness, kindness, and sentimentality took the place of truth, goodness, and love.

Nevertheless, they threw themselves into the local parish, Davy teaching Sunday School and the two of them working with young people at their home, the Studio reborn. But all was not well with Sheldon. He reports feeling restless, wanting a return to the shared life of beauty that was their pagan love. But his wife continued in her spiritual devotion, reading spiritual books, saying her prayers, reading Dom Julian's poems. A gap began to appear in their principle of sharing. Sheldon thought that in truth, Davy had a much deeper commitment to faith than he did. He viewed her as wanting sainthood, while he perhaps just wanted to be a Christian.

Was Davy onto the reality of faith? Maybe it's not constantly exciting, endlessly amusing, full of intellectual give and take, as they'd experienced Oxford. Perhaps Sheldon was confusing his academic experience with what he wanted from faith. Banners and pageantry don't exactly relate to one's ordinary neighbor.

Moreover, Sheldon notes that Davy was even becoming more "wifely," something he grew to detest. He even wished to have just one good fight, longing for the kind of relationship they'd had before. Was the Springtime of the past incompatible with their new faith? Was the old pagan joy in fact inconsistent with Christian religion? Must the Renaissance give way to Plymouth Rock?

What's especially curious, perhaps, is that they don't really discuss this problem directly. They don't call a Navigator's Council and work it all out. Does Christianity, in fact, destroy intimacy, does it shatter marriages? What happened to the notion that love fulfills all things?

Well, it got worse before things got better, as you know from the story, for Jane visited from England. And in Jane Sheldon found the old Davy's longing and joy. They shared so much together: poetry, art, music, and one another's souls. And then in the final night, they stayed up together nearly all night. Sheldon reports that he told Davy everything, but it didn't change the fact that he'd had an experience with Jane that seemed an awful lot like inloveness. In fact, he admits that he was in love with her. Maybe it didn't become a sexual relationship, but it was personally intimate.

How are we to evaluate this? Sheldon naturally feels very guilty and becomes even more impressed with his wife's virtue and his apparently pagan vice. But then something remarkable occurs on page 150. Have a look. They reconnect in their old way, remembering, re-loving, restoring one another's intimate trust. And somehow they both acquire the notion that God values their love too, that "we must hold the co-inherence of lovers *and* be Companions of the Co-inherence of the Incarnate Lord: she in me and I in her; Christ in us and we in Him." And then Sheldon adds a line from the First Epistle of St. John, the apostle of love: "Everyone who loves is the child of God." Love is *evidence* of the love of God. For all love is participation ultimately in divine love. They cannot be separated. Could it be that Davy's spirituality was the mistake?

Sheldon doesn't think so, and continues, "Perhaps that morning she came back for me and then perhaps, astonishingly, found herself further along the Way. At all events, joy flowered between us, the joy that I had thought to be pagan joy. After all, for Christian and unbeliever, there is but one spring of joy." Now, this is a remarkable statement. On the one hand, Sheldon endorses his constant view that Davy was more spiritual than he was and thus "came back" for him. On the other hand, he likewise endorses the view that the longing for "pagan" joy isn't "pagan" at all. Joy is joy, for all good things are found in God, because God made them all. The problem we are faced with is reconciling these two claims. If Sheldon was right all along, if his desire for intimate love of his wife through poetry, and books, and art, and conversation was *right*, then how could Davy have been right to reject all that in an effort to become more holy?

Let's approach this question another way: which is more holy, praying or washing the dishes? Be careful not to answer this one too quickly. The dishes do need to be washed, don't they? And what if it is your turn? Can you lay claim to a "higher spiritual duty" to pray? Or, to return to the Vanaukens' own case, suppose that Sheldon was interested in sex with Davy, and she begged off because she needed to read her Bible? Does that show great spirituality? Is sexual joy incompatible with divine joy? Don't the Christians, in fact, use sexual love as the highest, most intimate model of divine love?

If you are feeling confused, I should think that you would. Because Sheldon's view that Davy was so spiritual might just be wrong. And we don't get to see how their relationship might have evolved from what occurs on page 150, because she's in the hospital within just a few pages. Nor does one speak ill of the dead. So, perhaps this is as close as Sheldon will come to criticizing his wife. Plus, he feels great guilt over things with Jane. That's not unreasonable. But nor is Davy's repudiation of all natural beauties! You'd almost think she was trying to live as a nun.

Hmm . . . now there's an interesting thought, don't you think? After all, who was Davy's exemplar of a spiritual life? Was it an older, saintly married woman? That's what you might expect. But no, it was Dom Julian, a monk. And now we come to the crux of the question: if a married woman models her life on the alternative vocation of a monk, how is that going to work successfully? The love of God does not separate husband and wife, for it includes them both in their union. Sheldon was right about that. But this means that it is right for them to love intimately as man and wife. Marital love *is* spiritual.

The confusion all lies with the term "spiritual." Do we mean "spiritual" as opposed to "physical"? It sounds like it, if you look at the way in which Davy eschewed physical (pagan) joy for the sake of Bible reading and meditations. On this view, the non-physical, the incorporeal, i.e., is viewed as good, while the corporeal is viewed as bad. But this isn't the Christian view at all, for God made both corporeal and incorporeal and said of both that they were good. It's not the Christians but the Gnostics who identify good with incorporeality (substituting the ambiguous term "spiritual") and evil with corporeality. On the contrary, for historic Christianity both physical and spiritual are good. Both corporeal and incorporeal are "spiritual" (if by "spiritual" we mean *good*). For that is the ambiguity: does "spiritual" merely mean the opposite of "physical" or does it mean "good"? It the former, then being spiritual is *not* the objective of a human being. If the latter, then being spiritual is the objective of all persons, for goodness is our objective. The problem is that the Christian texts use the term *both* ways. You can see how this ambiguity helped the Gnostics infect early Christianity. But the ancient Christians also fiercely defended the fact that both physical and spirit are good, for human destiny is not to become a spirit, an angel. The promise within the Christian faith is the resurrection of the body and its full reunification with the soul for a completely restored human person.

So, we are led to the surprising conclusion that Davy became entrapped by Gnostic influences, once she returned to Virginia. And her devotion to Dom Julian's special form of monastic life confused her into thinking it was better for her to do religious devotionals than the poetry of John Donne. But all love is of God. All beauty points to divine beauty. All truth is God's truth. She withdrew from her marital life, and in so doing created the gap that Sheldon interpreted as his failure. And yes, he did fail not only in falling in love with Jane, but also in not realizing that his wife's apparently advanced spirituality was actually an illusion.

At least that's my take on the matter. Consider what you think. But whatever you conclude, you must take into account the remarkable re-unification between the two of them on page 150.

CHAPTER TWENTY

A SEVERE MERCY

(Sheldon Vanauken, *A Severe Mercy*, Chs. 7-10)

In our final chapter on *A Severe Mercy*, we want to consider C. S. Lewis' comment to Sheldon that Davy's death was "a severe mercy." We'll begin with the story of her death and then consider Lewis' evaluation. We left the narrative with Sheldon and Davy reconnecting in their inloveness, now not threatened by God, but realizing that God values all goods. No sooner did this occur, but the illness that Davy sensed a year before returns. Davy had the impression a year before that she was in trouble, and she prayed that she might be spared a year for her husband's and the group's sake. She got that year and attributed it to her prayer. Perhaps she was right. But now the year was up, and she is struck by some illness for which there is apparently no cure. Sheldon now dives into prayer for her sake, and his prayer for her is instructive on how much he has changed since his intellectual faith of the Oxford years. You might recall that his faith didn't seem fully human, as all-encompassing and influencing the entirety of his life. But now he offers God a deal.

Usually when we hear about deals offered to God, they are offered desperately and in ways that seem rather self-serving. I look over the hood of my car and see that it's moving toward the bridge edge. I'm trapped in my seat, facing certain death. "Oh God," I cry out, "save me, and I'll work in soup kitchens for the poor every single day!"

I suppose you'll laugh, certainly less than impressed with my sudden piety. Possibly God isn't impressed either. But Sheldon's prayer is different. He doesn't offer all kinds of wild promises if only God will give Davy back to him. His prayer isn't centered on *his* good at all. Instead, his prayer is for her sake, and only if it will do her a true good. He asks that God might take him instead of her. Think about how different that is from the usual selfish prayers of desperation. What does he get out of it for himself if God accepts the bargain? Nothing. It's not about him. It's for her sake. Sheldon characterizes this prayer as the most pure and unselfish act of all his life.

This also shows us that Sheldon's faith has matured significantly, doesn't it? For if the purpose of faith is to transform us into lovers, then Sheldon's love for his wife's true good shows a maturing faith. What's more, look how he acts for her benefit during her ordeal, even sharing her burden of worry and pain. Did you even think that could be possible? It's one of the most tantalizing elements of their story, that people so much in tune with one another can actually leave off an emotional burden for their partner to carry, confident that he will indeed carry it for her. She chose to give him her fear, and he chose to carry it for her. Is it possible that such choices can actually transfer the fear?

While Sheldon's life is finally directed "under the Obedience," Davy continues in her own love, late at night nursing the other patients through their agonies. And through it all she maintains her fundamental principle: all shall be most well. How does faith enable this kind of hope? Mull that over, for the

Christians are famous for saying that faith works through hope to effect love. Are they right?

On page 164 Sheldon offers us a unique insight into the motivating principle of their lives now that Christianity has reformed the Shining Barrier. He tells us that love lies at the bottom of all things, its power greater than evil, for it alone is the final reality. Be mindful that he says this as his wife moves toward her death. And it's just in and through such experiences that we human beings love, isn't it? Love isn't just some abstract ideal, but something to be *done*. And it is done through time, as a habit. That's why we call it a virtue. Whether our lives work out very well, or whether we encounter vast disappointments and trouble, we can still learn to love, can't we?

After her death Sheldon is struck by the absolute conviction that Davy *is*. Not a partial Davy, a Davy of this or that day, but a whole Davy completed from all the Davys that he had loved in her temporal life. It's a remarkable idea, that we are becoming who we are. Unlike the angels, we choose in tiny little bits, here and there, for though we are possessed of spirit, of some immaterial component that both philosophers and theologians call "soul," we are also body spread out in time and space. And so we sleep and then wake, we fast and then feast, we yearn for Spring to complete the cycle of the seasons that will start yet again. Our lives are filled with these peaks and troughs, and through them and in them we choose and we form who we are, our character, the true self that we are becoming. In death our formation is complete. We even remember the dead in that way, eulogizing their lives, having gathered all the person together in our imaginations. But Sheldon thinks that it's more than mere imagination.

He offers to strengthen that conviction for us by relating to us the intense dream he had of Davy following her death. Davy returned from death to assure him that she was all right, that all was most well. These kinds of experiences are reported by many people at the deaths of loved ones, not just in dreams either, but sometimes in fully veridical experience. But it helps confirm his confidence that immortality is real, that what religion aims us toward is a genuine completion of the human person.

After some time passed, Sheldon's relationship with Lewis grew to the point that he felt comfortable relating to Lewis the full story behind the Shining Barrier. Lewis took a dim view toward the project, as you can tell from the letter he wrote back to Sheldon. Let's take a look at what Lewis said.

He offers Sheldon a multilayered view of how the human family throughout time would look on the Shining Barrier. He starts with the grosser Pagans, the ancient polytheistic folk. They would say that the excess in such love would provoke the jealousy of the gods. How dare mortals lay claim to immortal love? And with that jealousy would come the retribution we discover in the ancient myths. As for the finer Pagans, such as Aristotle, they would say that the Shining Barrier sought to make love solely for its own sake, leaving out all the other duties of man, such as civic duty, or same gender friendships. You might have thought about this too. How does their early relationship do anyone else any good? Moreover, doesn't it tend to limit the very different kinds of friendships that males form with one another and that females form with one another? Coming to the Stoics, Lewis notes that the entire project of the Shining Barrier would be rejected as plain contrary to nature, since they'd see it as an attempt to turn a part into the whole. Their love was supposed to be a part of the human family, not sufficient unto itself. It never could have satisfied them, if it had been left so isolated, so sterile. Just imagine two lovers stranded on an island. In spite of the most glorious love between them, is that really enough for what we think of as fully human experience?

Lewis now moves to the Christians, and sees them as advancing the same themes already developed, that yes, marital love is good in itself, but it is also good for other things, namely God, neighbor, and the children it ought to have produced. Lewis thinks that Sheldon deprived Davy of maternal virtues and experience, a loss that might be of far more significance to a woman than the loss of paternity might be for a man. The very notion that their experiences in life were somehow fully shareable was itself ridiculous, for though lovers learn to see the world through the eyes of their beloved, they never possess those same eyes. Lewis appeals to sex as a case in point. Sexual experiences of a man and a woman are not shareable. Neither party can get into the other one's head and understand the experience. Nor could Sheldon understand what it was like for Davy to abandon maternity.

Let's try to understand what Lewis is saying here. Love between two people is not supposed to make them into one another. It's a relation of differences, not a transformation of two into one identity. Love, in fact, depends very much on reciprocal and differing powers employing their special capabilities on the lacks that are found in the beloved. This very much fits into the traditional view of the way in which the genders relate differently to one another, each possessing capabilities that the other gender lacks and finds completed through the loving care of the other.

Lewis isn't rejecting the notion that lovers should share their lives together, but the idea that *everything* can be shared is simply false. And it proved false in ways that brought Davy and Sheldon to deprive themselves of experiences that in fact might have significantly enhanced not only their virtue but their love for one another. Parents know what a transformation children produce in their lives, both in their love for one another and in their love for their children. Good parenting requires the most supreme effort and, thereby, develops mature human virtues. Some even say that you don't really grow up until you have children.

Lewis goes on to say that their love was an attempt to prevent the natural growth cycle of love. Perpetual springtime is not allowed. He doesn't mean by this that all couples must fall out of love and become cruel to one another. Rather, he means that all mortal loves must be taken up into charity for their fulfillment or else they will be depended upon to bring a fulfillment for the person that they cannot hope to do. No mortal love can do for a person what only divine love can.

So, Lewis thinks they were treated to a kind of mercy, even if severe. Her death prevented the (perhaps horrible) death of their relationship, since it could not have ultimately produced what they were hoping for, at least not in the way that they had set it up in the Shining Barrier. That disappointment would eventually have led them to trouble. Lewis' view assumes that love, just like human happiness, is a real thing, and if you don't act according to the true pattern of human fulfillment, you just won't be fulfilled. We sometimes hear the claim that love and fulfillment are different for everyone, that you can do whatever you like and still be happy. Serial killers do that, but are they fulfilled? Ever met a serial killer? These are seriously dark people, void of human feeling, empty shells of what they should have been. Fulfilled? None of the ancient philosophers and certainly not the Christians either ever thought that happiness was just getting everything you want regardless of what it is. You have to want the right things, and more than that, happiness goes way beyond want-fulfillment. Happiness is the highest state of a human being, our *best* state. It follows that happiness must be complete human virtue. You don't get that by mass murder. And you don't get that by fabricating novel theories of love that don't accord with human nature either. Love and happiness are *real*, that's the point, but it means that they have a genuine structure and order and nature to them. You don't follow it properly, you miss out.

Let's move on to Sheldon's reaction to this letter. You can imagine how you'd react. Most of us would probably be so furious we'd tear it up. But Sheldon was used to being honest with himself, part of the virtue necessary to be a Christian. Though he rejects what Lewis said about children and seems dubious about the notion that perpetual springtime might not be allowed, he had to admit that their love would eventually have led to one of three consequences if it had continued unreformed. The first possibility he mentions is that he should have become as faithful to God as Davy. But Sheldon has doubts about how strong his commitment really was then. We'll have to let him be the judge of his own heart. The second possibility is that he might have come to resent her faith and as such might have tried to lessen her commitment. That would have undermined rather than fulfilled her good; how is that love? Third, he worries that he might have come truly to hate Davy in a kind of jealousy of God. And then there would have been other Janes, only not so innocent. This spiral effect down into true disaster brought him to the realization that maybe in a strange way it was a kind of mercy—though severe—for Davy to die before any of these horrors had time to mature.

Reflect on whether you think Davy's death was a severe mercy or not. Do you think Lewis is right? Do you think Sheldon fully understood what Lewis was saying?

Finally, we often hear about people losing their faith through difficult circumstances. But loss and grief are sometimes the nurturing ground of faith. Ask yourself how philosophy itself could fare in these circumstances. Does religion offer something else? Is there any hope in philosophy? If not, and if religion does have something more, why is this the case?

CHAPTER TWENTY-ONE

THE PROBLEM OF EVIL

(David Hume, *Dialogues Concerning Natural Religion*, Parts X-XI)

Our reading for today returns us to traditional philosophy to confront one of the most famous problems in thinking about the existence and nature of God: the problem of evil. Hume's book presents three characters in dialogue—Demea, Cleanthes, and Philo. Demea and Cleanthes are theists, though different varieties, while Philo appears more skeptical. Initially, one gets the impression that Philo agrees with Demea's view that difficulty or grief in the world motivates religious thought and devotion. But quickly it becomes apparent that Philo is no true ally to Demea but is instead permitting Demea to make the case for the great amount of trouble in the world not to inspire us toward greater piety, but instead to suddenly turn the argument against the view that God is really all that loving. How can a good God permit evil in the world without doing something to stop it? It would seem that he is strong enough to prevent evil (if he is omnipotent). It would also seem that he is knowledgeable enough to prevent evil (if he is omniscient). Likewise, it would seem that he would wish to prevent evil (if he is omnibenevolent). Yet, evil exists. So, either God is not omniscient, or he is not omnipotent, or he is not omnibenevolent.

If you recall our metaphysical treatment of God's nature, you'll probably remember that once you arrive at one infinite attribute, say omnipotence, e.g., you can derive the other ones. They are, as we like to say in logic, mutually entailing. But that also means that if you lose one, you lose them all. Thus, the full force of the problem of evil isn't that God might lose an attribute here or there, but rather, that if evil exists, then God doesn't.

In evaluating the argument, you might have noticed that the conclusion is fairly strong in its logical force. It's not saying that God probably doesn't exist. It's not even saying that God merely doesn't exist. It's going one step further in claiming that God cannot exist in a world with evil in it. Thus, this argument seeks to demonstrate that God and evil are incompatible, as contradictory together as a square circle.

You might think that we can dispense with the force of this argument by just getting rid of evil. Perhaps evil isn't in the world or even in our action, but merely in how we look at the world. Perhaps it's just a matter of perception. If you look more closely at events like volcanic eruptions, you might think that they actually do the world a great amount of good in the long run. So, volcanic destruction is merely the illusion of evil. In fact, it's good.

Well, this argument might appear cogent at first, but we do run into a few problems. First, what if you are one of the people overcome by volcanic ash and lava . . . imagining all the good that volcanic nutrients will do the soil in a few decades probably doesn't make your death worth it to you, does it? Second, philosophers distinguish evil into two kinds, natural evils like volcanic eruptions, and moral evils like murders and political corruption and sloth. It's much harder to see how the harmful things that we do to one another can be written off as an illusion. Are we to believe that genocidal actions only *seem* to be evil, but on the greater scheme of things they really are good? Wasn't that exactly the sort of argument the Nazis used to justify getting rid of what they thought of as lesser races, in order to promote a future much better for the allegedly pure race? And even if sometimes good things can be worked out of bad actions, such as when a domestic abuse case finally separates two people allowing the innocent party to rebuild his life, this doesn't make the original abuse *good*, does it?

So, it looks like we'll have to admit that evil isn't an illusion, but that lands us back in the dilemma. Apparently, something has to go, God or evil. But maybe we're moving too fast. Do we really think that God and evil are incompatible? Is there no situation in which God might permit evil? I mean, don't parents allow their children some latitude in order to learn to make up their own minds? In fact, couldn't we argue that moral freedom *requires* non-interference? If God intervened in our lives so that every time I tried to stab you with a knife, it turned into butter, then the action of murder would itself become impossible. And if God did that for every evil action, then the very notion of a fixed natural medium between us would prove incoherent. I mean, if the natural world is real, then it mustn't change when we try to act on it. The same hill that provides sledding joy for me provides a hurdle for you as you try to climb it! Without a fixed natural medium, creatures like ourselves wouldn't be possible.

But I suppose the most compelling point here is that continual divine interference would undermine our capacity to love. You might wonder about that, thinking that surely a world where everyone loves everyone else would be just great! So, why doesn't God just fix everything and turn us into that world? Let's imagine that he did that, changing all of us, so that we always love one another. We'd be slaves to God wouldn't we? Can love be enslaved? If your father drags you up to the altar in chains and hands you off to the groom, is that a real marriage? Or do we think instead that real love must be freely offered and freely accepted? If so, it *must* be possible to say, "No."

The strange reality is that God cannot create a universe of persons (free agents) who automatically love him. Freedom means that some of the persons might choose to reject his love. And he has to accept that if he's going to make us free. Now, he didn't have to make us free, did he? No, he didn't. But the universe is much richer with free agents in it, isn't it? Don't you prefer to be a person, say, than a worm? Isn't the capacity to love and create far better? Surely freedom is better than slavery.

So, where does this leave us? It appears from the foregoing argument that we cannot just assume that God would intervene to prevent evil. In fact, we can go so far as to say that he would not intervene to prevent evil, if he creates free creatures. Love is just that valuable. The upshot of this discussion is that evil and God are not incompatible after all. Granted, God cannot *be* evil. In that sense, there is incompatibility. But in the sense that the problem of evil is raising, namely how could a good God not interfere to stop evil, there is no incompatibility. God and evil are possible in the same universe, namely in a universe where God creates free agents, persons like ourselves.

In one sense, you might think it a bit audacious of us to turn our fury against God, especially when most of the evil that we complain about is what we do to one another. Why don't we just behave? Moreover, you can just imagine the resentment we'd all feel if God constantly intervened to "fix" things for us. We sort of think of this as *our* world. The religious traditions endorse that view by telling us that God gave it to us. So, what are we complaining about? If we really want a good world, why don't we act properly toward one another? It won't do to blame God.

But there's still something bothersome about the problem of evil. Let's take the parental image again. Aren't there some things that parents *do* intervene in? Such as a child's reporting thoughts on suicide? And if God presents himself to us as Father, then shouldn't we expect fatherly intervention at least now and then?

I suppose someone might say that God does intervene. Don't we have all sorts of reports of answered prayers, and angelic rescues, and miracles? Perhaps we do, and for the sake of this argument, let's suppose that *all* those reports are true (asking too much, probably). That still leaves us with all the cases where there is no rescue, where the murderer isn't stopped, where the bombers just keep coming . . . why doesn't God intervene then? In fact, if God intervenes at all, it makes you wonder why he doesn't intervene more? If he just followed a general rule of non-intervention, then we might understand it, as a commitment to our freedom. But the religious traditions say that he intervenes. Where does that leave us?

Let's back up and compare the original form of the problem of evil to the very different form we're considering now. The incompatibility version said that God and evil cannot possibly coexist. But we saw that they surely can, namely in any case where God creates free persons. But now we're considering a different version of the problem, the one that Philo ultimately settles on in our reading. On this version, God and evil aren't said to be incompatible. Their compatibility is granted. The problem here is that there just seems to be too much evil to think that the universe was created by or is run by a benevolent creator. The incompatibility version of the problem requires that there be *no* evil. The improbability version of the problem requires that there be far *less* evil. The greater the evil we find in the world (either because God made a flawed system to begin with, or because God doesn't intervene to stop it), the less likely it seems that a benevolent creator exists. You can see that this argument reduces the likelihood or probability that God exists in direct proportion to the amount of evil that we discover in the world.

I suppose we might wonder about the new premise of this second form of the problem of evil. Is it really the case that there's just too much evil in the world? Cleanthes tries to rebut Philo's argument by suggesting that there is a great amount of good in the world too. Just consider your morning. You awaken in a *bed*. Do you put your feet onto cold concrete? No, nice soft carpet. You turn on the coffee pot. You smell the coffee. You drink the coffee. You drink more coffee. You open the window and the birds are singing, the flowers are in bloom, the sun dazzles your groggy eyes. The world is full of goods, if we only open our eyes. If we were to compare the number of goods to the number of evils, can we really believe that the evils could outweigh the goods?

Philo admits that there are an awful lot of goods in the world. Perhaps we should appreciate them more. But are all goods and all evils equivalent? As I'm putting goods and evils onto the scales, is the delight of drinking a cup of coffee of equal weight to the horror of suffering a physical assault? You see, Philo is concerned that though goods may well outweigh evils in quantity, evils may outweigh goods considered qualitatively.

This is where the Holocaust usually comes into the argument, doesn't it? The qualitative losses that these people experienced don't get better merely by surviving the camps, and moving to America or Israel, and starting a new life. But we're probably being selective in our choices of events, focusing overly much on our own era. The truth is that mass slaughters have been the stuff of history from the beginnings of human civilization. But that doesn't make things better for Cleanthes' argument, does it? There's an awful lot of evil in our history, and qualitatively, it's a true horror.

Maybe we are being too selective, though. For as we find these moments of despairing destruction, don't we also have to admit that most of the time people live their lives in relative calm and peace? That their joys in life make life worth living? If we all thought that doom was all we had to look forward to, if life was that bad, wouldn't we just end it all? But we keep going, and we keep hoping, and we keep believing that it's not going to be that bad in the end. We believe that *we* can do something to make it better.

And maybe therein lies part of the solution to this problem. The evils we're referring to in order to make the qualitative case for evil are *moral* evils, the evils that we commit against one another. But we can stop doing this. We can make a better world. How can we blame God for what we do to one another? God didn't kill the people in the Holocaust. We did. And he didn't stop it either. But we did. Perhaps that's the point. Maybe our notion of all this divine intervention is the problem. Maybe our actions have real consequences on other people, and God is not going to create the illusion that it really doesn't matter. It's just too easy to shove the responsibility for what we do or fail to do onto God.

CHAPTER TWENTY-TWO

QUILTED RELIGION

(Thomas Howard, *Christ the Tiger*, Parts 1-2)

We're now moving on to our second narrative in our look at religious experience. In the case of the Vanaukens, we saw people who grew up outside the religious tradition and really wanted nothing to do with it. But faith had a way of finding them. In Thomas Howard's case, faith was all that he knew growing up. He was immersed in religious culture, only he eventually longed to escape it.

One of the thematic questions for our reflections in this book is this question: what is religion *for*? What end does it serve? What good is achieved through it? Howard's autobiographical narrative offers us some new answers to this question. So, let's begin with the religious milieu in which Howard was born. What were they like? What were they trying to achieve?

Howard describes his earliest memories as focused on the desire for safety, order, and security. Religion provided a filter for him to avoid the harsh outside world. Howard sought a kind of religious coziness, in which conformity to well-defined roles enabled an idealized kind of life. Howard's faith was characterized essentially by inner piety. But that piety was expressed through rituals of separation from the less pious people around him, not only unbelievers, but even other Christian groups that lacked the level of commitment and zeal that characterized Howard's group. He was immersed in a culture of spiritual greatness, fed on the heroes of the Bible, told that he too must be a Moses, an Elijah, a Daniel, doing great things for God. And so, his culture tended to identify certain vocations as those that were "for God" and others as less significant, less spiritual. To enter the ministry, to become a missionary to the heathen abroad, these were the activities that earned community (and thus, divine) praise. Other vocations, such as joining a rock and roll band or becoming a tattoo artist, would only have earned censure, since those kinds of people didn't live according to true spirituality.

Howard tried hard to fulfill the expectations of his religious culture, so much so, that he almost out-spiritualized them at their own game. Those of you familiar with the New Testament might see a parallel between the early Howard and the early St. Paul (when he was known as Saul the Pharisee). Both men zealously sought to consistently apply the principles of their systems, beyond what most of their practitioners did. When Howard headed to a Christian college, for example, he found a variety of groups vying for the claim to true spirituality. Howard participated in the special form of faith that he found in each one, trying desperately to satisfy the inner drive for authentic spirituality. But in each case he was left despondent, feeling that whatever animated the members failed to capture him.

Howard felt most moved aesthetically, by artistic objects, but not by things approved by his religious culture. So, he felt guilty for liking them, but couldn't shake the feeling that somehow faith ought not to feel fear, for example, of the depiction of a chaotic human mind. What finally opened Howard's world was his military service. There he found people as unlike him as an Amazonian native is from someone working on Wall Street. But he *liked* them. He felt that he had finally encountered human beings just being human. For all their faults, for all their failure to conform to his religious codes, for all their unbelief, it was their humanity that drew him. And that raised a question for him, didn't it? What good is a form of religion that cuts one off from human experience? Is faith supposed to hide one from the world outside? Is religion really a return to the womb?

On pages 82ff, Howard describes his feelings about taboo religion, about forms of faith that offer a haven of protection from the outside world. The objective, he thought, was to outgod God, by creating a series of rules and expectations that prevented one from ever getting near acting badly. If you want to avoid lust, then board up the adult book stores, show only rated G movies, censure women whose bodily shape can be seen through their clothing, prohibit make-up, require that all women wear their hair in a bun, and, for that matter, have all women wear prairie dresses! In this way, the *thought* of sexuality won't occur, and thus, the action can be avoided. Sounds kind of like that Fundamentalist Latter Day Saints cult, doesn't it?

But Howard thought that maybe sex was actually good. Hmm . . .

In another example, he offers us the problem that wine posed for people of his religious subculture. Wine made people drunk, turned men on their families, left women on the streets selling themselves to make ends meet; it was a pernicious liquid that needed to be banned to safeguard civilization! Yet Jesus made six huge pots of it for his first miracle. And the communion ceremony in the church uses bread and wine. Maybe it's not the wine that's the problem, but the way in which it is used?

Yes, that's what Howard concluded. *Things* are not evil. They can't be, since God created all things and said that they were good. *Actions* are what can be evil. But you cannot safeguard people' moral choices by prohibiting access to the things. Yes, if you allow alcohol in your community, some people will abuse it. But alcohol also serves many good uses, if used properly. Yes, if you praise the enjoyment of sexual love, some people will try to separate the sex from the love. But sexual love isn't a bad thing. God made it.

We've run into this kind of thing before, haven't we? Doesn't Howard's experience sound Gnostic to you? Physical things are classified as evil, while abstaining from the things makes one spiritual? This is the classic Gnostic dichotomy of identifying good with immateriality and evil with the physical. But physical things are good. Howard finally realizes that the Incarnation of God as a man into the world ratifies the status of nature. For how could God become a man if man was bad? Of course, the ancient Gnostics rejected the very idea that God had become incarnate from the Virgin Mary. Some said that God merely passed through her without actually touching her body. Others said that the "Christ" only fell on Jesus at his baptism, and then hastily left just before the crucifixion (leaving the guy Jesus hanging out on a limb—couldn't resist the pun). Modern day Gnostics of the Christian kind tend to avoid making these classically absurd religious claims, but they nevertheless maintain the Gnostic ethic with its fundamental assertion that the purpose of religion is to enable us to escape human nature.

Howard is moved by humanity on deeply imaginative grounds. Not just the pretty pictures, and the knightly castles, and the puppies, but by the darkness and anxiety and terror and horror that real human beings actually endure. His faith seemed unable to cope with those realities, so it created defensive walls of separation to avoid them. But Howard says that Jesus, the hero of all the Christians, smashed all such walls. He walked with and talked with real people, even the people that the Gnostics of his day said no one should talk to, such as the Samaritan woman. Jesus was alive and sinewy and human, while Howard's faith was brittle, dull, and frightened.

Howard's worries did not just extend to the moral requirements of his culture, but also to their epistemic ones. He noticed that one just did not ask the obvious question: what if we are *wrong*? Doubt was not encouraged (though guilt was apparently okay). Certain things had to be taken on faith. God was big enough to protect his own people. Yes, perhaps, but *are* we his people? How do we know? What if we are the prodigal son? What if we are the faithless Israelites? What if we are the Pharisees that Jesus condemns? Howard notes that it was just a given that the test of authenticity and truth was the level of one's sincerity. How could their zeal and purity have derived from anything other than the truth? Well, you might recall that Locke noted that "intractable zealots" full of sincerity can nevertheless oppose one another, showing that sincerity is no guarantee of authenticity.

Finally, all these aesthetic, moral, and epistemic elements came together for Howard in the attempt by members of his community to see the world through rosy lenses. If horrors happened out in the world, they had to be accepted as God's will. Apparently, God too had to be safeguarded from the realities of the world. At funerals one couldn't weep and wail, for God sovereignly determined that person's death, so one should instead focus on the happiness of the future blessed day. Howard sums up the problem on the bottom of page 111:

> I belonged to a tradition that affirmed the idea of Love and not havoc as lying at the bottom of things. The data of human experience lead one, however, to quite an opposite conclusion. And yet we claimed that this Love is knowable and operative—indeed, definitive—in human existence. But in our eagerness to substantiate this claim, we were forced to respond to experience with visionary imagery that often did violence to human sensibilities.

We find ourselves facing the challenge of evil again, don't we? Only now Howard is questioning Vanauken's assertion that love rather than havoc lies at the bottom of all things. Which is it? Mull that one for a while before we rejoin Howard in our next chapter.

CHAPTER TWENTY-THREE

TRANSFIGURATION

(Thomas Howard, *Christ the Tiger*, Part 3)

In our last chapter, we looked at Howard's experience growing up in a dogmatic religious world which aimed at security, comfort, insularity, and the conviction of divinely special status. In the last section of Howard's book, he portrays three additional visions of life beyond the dogmatist vision: the hedonist vision, the secularist vision, and the transfigurative vision.

Let's begin with the hedonist vision. Howard rejected the dogmatic religious view of the world, because it sought to hide from reality, and if religion has any claim to being true, he became convinced that it had to make sense of experience. The hedonist vision ratifies experience, for according to Howard, it is more than just the pursuit of pleasure (the usual definition of hedonism). Rather it involves all that beauty and goodness that is located in music, the arts, and literature, namely the life of the imagination. Howard sought to acquire all kinds of imaginative experience in an effort to validate and authentic his experience, in effect, to bring meaning and significance to his life. The hedonist vision ratifies reality, because it acknowledges the powerful draw of the world around us, recognizing the goodness that must lie there. Howard's city life illustrates this kind of pursuit, the ever-driving chase after new kinds of experience in film, fashion, literature, conversation, sexuality, politics, art, and music. It looks at human culture and recognizes the creative impulse that drives it as positive.

But the hedonist vision failed Howard for three important reasons. First, it didn't ultimately satisfy him; there was always some new experience promising to arrive. What's more, who can possibly acquire all experiences from all the different histories and cultures in the world? Collecting experiences isn't all that different than collecting anything else. How does the collection satisfy a human being? If we are nothing but desire, then I suppose it should do a pretty good job. But we aren't just desires. Second, what makes experiences so valuable (and Howard thinks that they are good) is when they provide the forum for love between people, the loves of friendship, *eros*, and families. It's great to see the Grand Canyon, but isn't it better to do so with the people you love? Love is greater than experience collection. Third, a full reconciliation with reality requires that one confront not just the pleasures of life, but also the pain, irrevocability, despair, death, and loss that Howard depicts so forcefully. Hedonism isn't any better than religious dogmatism at dealing with the ugly side of life. It tries at first to ignore it, and then actively evade it, and in the end opts for some kind of escapism (drug addiction, attempts to reclaim lost youth through tummy tucks, etc.) that is distinct from but similar to the dogmatic pursuit of heaven as an escape into a realm of pure spirit. All forms of escapism try to take us out of the pain by ultimately denying our nature.

Howard next turns to what he calls the secularist vision. This is the tinkerist vision, the life of the volunteer, social organizer, and political activist. On this view of life, the problems that Howard describes can be answered by social action. Human existence can be reformed to minimize the inequalities and harms that people suffer. Eden can be reclaimed from myth as the goal of a brave new world, a great society that corrects the errors of the past and finally brings home utopia. But this vision also fails Howard, not least because he doesn't seem all that comfortable with people! The ancient philosophers and religious folk both would have thought of this as the worst pipedream. The old vision saw that utopia was the realm of the gods, not mortal men. When men try to create towers able to reach heaven, those towers always fall, killing a good many of the builders. Why? Because no matter how well you form your society, with the perfect constitution, the best set of laws, and the best representatives of the people, you cannot ever create a system so perfect that nobody will have to be good. Social form can never replace individual ethics. You might recall Socrates' dispute with Meletus who claimed that his sophistical educative system could guarantee virtue. But Socrates believed that true education, dialectic, must be sought by the student himself. Goodness cannot be forced, but must be freely chosen. As such, no social order can guarantee virtue. And therefore, no amount of political reform can guarantee happiness.

But Howard sees something right in the secularist vision too, the recognition that Eden mattered, that we must be moving toward our complete good. The problem is reconciling the mimetic and mythic visions. The mythic vision recognizes the greatness within human destiny, affirms the good of human nature, and longs for its full restitution. But the mimetic demands an accounting for our actual condition, for it draws and paints and sings and writes about all that darkness and despair and frustration and loss and decay that Howard so eloquently portrays. How can we acknowledge both? How can we seek the highest splendor in a way that acknowledges the force of its loss?

The secularist seeks to overcome the gap first by flattening it out. He settles for less and claims that that will suffice for happiness. The secularist, secondly, forces people to join the movement. He knows what's good for them, and so he compels their commitment. This is the well-known result of ideologists of all stripes. Invariably, whether they represent the political right or the political left, they are always trying to find ways to coerce the people into conforming to their ideological pattern. But the sword never made anybody good.

Howard thinks that the gap can be crossed, but not by flattening the difference between the mimetic and the mythic. We hear the call of Mount Olympus, the realm of the gods, and know that somehow our destiny lies in that Court. But at the same time we acknowledge the awful realities that prevent our ascension to immortal happiness. The gap must be acknowledged, must be admitted to. It cannot be rejected, evaded, ignored, or flattened as the other three visions all attempt, cheating in one way or another.

Then how is it to be crossed? Howard's answer might be surprising, because he returns to religion, only this time not so dogmatic and brittle. For he sees in the figure of Christ that the gap was crossed not by us, but by him. What if God should come down from Olympus, suffering with our agonies, to show us a way of love that transcends anything we've been able to achieve through dogmatism, hedonism, or secularism? In the (anti-Gnostic) Christian incarnation, Howard thinks the mythic is made fact and offers the promise to finally wholly overcome the real loss and suffering that people endure. Jesus didn't placate people in their suffering. He *healed* them. Howard thinks that what is necessary to make things right goes far beyond mere compensation, all the way to full redemption—the transfiguration and reordering of all things in the love of God. This is called charity, *caritas* in Latin. But it cannot be ordered by the sword. It can only be offered and received freely, according to the mode of love.

Howard asks isn't this just pie in the sky wishful thinking? Is there any reason to think this might be true? His answer is that at some point the mythic hope of religion must become real, or else it is indeed just a ghastly cheat. And in the figure of Jesus he thinks it actually happened.

CHAPTER TWENTY-FOUR

A CHALLENGE TO THE GODS

(C. S. Lewis, *Till We Have Faces*, Pages 1-76)

Till We Have Faces is very probably the most complex work we'll discuss in this book, which is part of the reason why we've saved it until the end. But because it's a story, you might have the misimpression that it's easy going. Pay close attention to the details as you read it, especially the imagery and symbolism—for example, the roles that face and facelessness play throughout the book. The book becomes especially complex in Part II, so my usual recommendation is to just take the plunge and read through the entire novel all the way through first. Then go back and read each of these chapters as you re-read the novel. This strategy is especially useful because, once you have a sense of where the book is going, you'll notice important details during the reread.

That being said, what is this book about? It's about human frustration with gods. Yes, you heard me right—plural, gods. This book is entirely pagan, in that the religious structure is polytheistic, very much like what you would have found throughout the ancient world prior to the rise of Christianity. But for all that, it doesn't mean we don't have anything to learn. Even if you are a monotheist and a Christian to boot, your own theology makes space for the gap between God and men. We talked about that when we discussed the angels. Also, remember that the source of a truth is irrelevant to whether it is true. It doesn't matter where a good argument comes from, just that it's good; pagans can teach us true things too. Moreover, the early Christians quickly realized that they owed a great deal to their religious and philosophical forefathers, not just the Jews, and not just Socrates and the Greek philosophers, but even pagan religion. Granted, they thought that much of pagan religion was seriously confused. But they already appreciated that truth emerges through imagery.

Finally, don't forget that Lewis is very probably the most influential Christian thinker of the twentieth century, even though so much of what he contributed theologically was meant for more popular audiences. Lewis brought the medieval mind alive for modern Christians, reminding them of the ancient faith that he cleverly called "mere" Christianity. So, Lewis is using the old myth of Psyche and Cupid in order to tell another story, what the Greeks would have familiarly called a "re-telling." The Greeks had contests among their playwrights to determine who could re-tell the old tales the best. We do something similar in the film industry, when every twenty years or so the same script is given a makeover and a remake is born. Lewis is going to stick to the general parameters of the old myth (and if you look at the note at the conclusion of his book, he'll briefly describe the original), but significantly expand on the story and even refocus our attention on another character, Orual. And, as you might expect from Lewis, what he takes from the old myth will be crucially important for our understanding of the new.

The theme of this book lies in the question Orual asks at the beginning, what do the gods want with us? Are we nothing but their playthings? She is old, she is a queen, and she is furious at the way in which she thinks she was manipulated and used by the god of the mountain. She writes this book, as she says in the opening paragraphs, no longer afraid of what the gods might do to her in retaliation. She is too old for plagues, terrors, or threats. Nor are threats and plagues an answer. That's what she wants—some accounting from the gods for their actions. An audacious plan, perhaps, but then she thinks she has quite the case. Part I of the book is her presentation of her case, in the form of the narrative of her life, especially her life with her dearest sister, Psyche. But as she will explain at the beginning of Part II, her writing Part I proved to be the beginnings of the gods' case against *her*. So, while you read Part I, pay very close attention to the details relevant to her argument with the gods. Is she right? Do you buy it? And remember, too, that we're only getting her side of the story. Vices don't just corrupt our conduct; they infect our imaginings and even our perception, so that over time we bend the world to make it fit what we decide it must be. (You've probably noticed that no one ever thinks that what he's doing is *really* wrong, for if he believed that seriously, he'd change. No, we always find a way to *justify* our behavior. And that often requires radically reconstructing events and motives to suit our justification.)

Let's begin our reflections on the book by comparing the three major influences on Orual, namely, her father the King, the old priest of Ungit, and the Fox her Greek slave-tutor. First, the King. The king is a man lacking in reflection. He feels, he acts, and he tends to act with respect to his self-interest alone. Keeping his political power intact is his major preoccupation, and things haven't been going well of late. As such, he is agitated, often angry, and flies into rages that lead him toward actions he might have thought better of had he thought at all. Though Orual is actually a fairly reflective person, she bears the King's blood in her body, and, along with it, his ill temper.

Secondly, let's talk about the Fox. The Fox is a Greek, captured in battle and sold to the barbarians of Glome. As such, he is one of the few who are literate and educated. His talents are recognized, and he becomes tutor to the girls and, eventually, advisor to the King. He is also a philosopher, a Stoic, to be precise. As you read the text, note the things he says about our relationship to the "divine nature," and what he says about the gods. Stoics tend to view the world as though most of it is a play already written. Our role is to play our part the best we can. We cannot change the events, but, if we learn to adapt to them, we can avoid misery and secure some measure of happiness. The Fox tends to be naturalistic in his outlook, meaning that he represents the beginnings of modern science. He thinks about the world and the gods in terms of evidence and reason. As such, he has little use for myth except for its beauty which occasionally captures him and makes him long for the Greeklands he left behind. The Fox loves Psyche and Orual. They come to call him "grandfather," and he is the major philosophical influence on Orual.

Finally, we come to the old Priest. The Priest represents the goddess Ungit who emerged from the earth as a large faceless stone. Her son is the god of the mountain. The religion of Ungit is a typically dark religion in which the gods are hidden behind curtains, clouds of incense, and darkness. You'll find the same thing through all pre-Christian religion (even Judaism) with the one exception of Akhenaten's worship of the god, Aten. The main Egyptian deity Amun's name means "hidden." It's worth asking yourself why the gods remain hidden from us. That's part of what Orual demands to know.

The religion of Ungit is also sacrificial, a religion of blood and death. For people in a post-Christian culture, blood religions strike us as barbaric and irrational. But Christianity is itself a blood religion that emerged out of Judaism—also (prior to the Roman destruction of the Temple sacrificial system) a blood religion. In fact, all religion was bloody and sacrificial. Rather than condemning it, we might first seek to understand it, for the text reports that the gods will have their sacrifices, they will have man. Why do we need to approach the gods through sacrifice and blood?

The religion of Ungit is also rooted in the human senses. Did you notice how Lewis tries to depict the smell, sound, and look of the old priest? He's old and gnarly, he wears the bird mask emblem, he carries the dried bladder rattles, and the reek and smell of Ungit is all about him—what Orual describes as the smell of holiness. It's difficult to give you an impression of just what this is like, but perhaps you might think about a high Christian mass on a major feast day like Easter. There you'll find the priests decked out in their most glorious vestments, the choir chanting, candlelight everywhere, and copious clouds of incense wafting around the altar. And that incense has the old smell too. Everyone in the ancient world knew that the holy smell was frankincense. If you've never smelled this substance burning as incense, you're missing out. It's an unforgettable smell, and you'll immediately think, "Oooooh, *that* smell, the smell of holiness." In the ancient world, you'd have to mix up blood and burned sacrificial flesh in order to get the whole picture.

What's the upshot of all this? Ungit is an earthy religion, deeply grounded in mystery, myth, darkness, and blood. And for all that, perhaps even because of all that, it works for the people very well, even if they are incredibly superstitious.

Orual is thus formed by a mixture of the religion of Ungit and the philosophy of Fox, not to mention her genetic heritage from her father. She is the only one in Glome caught between world views. Psyche is another story entirely.

Let's address Orual's sisters. Redival, the eldest, is pretty (she has her curls), lusty, and pretty much a buffoon. Psyche comes last and is the picture of Beauty herself, but, for all that, she is possessed of an extraordinary virtue and deeply sensitive heart. Orual functions as a mother as well as a sister to Psyche, something critical to Orual's identity, because she is very probably the ugliest person in all of Glome. Her father thinks she's useless, because she'll never be available for marriage, so he finally settles on requiring the Fox to teach Orual philosophy, figuring that if he can teach Orual, a mere girl, then when finally a son is born to the royal house, there's a good chance that the Fox will be able to educate him well.

The central thrust of the storyline occurs after Istra—Psyche is her Greek name—steps out to touch the people during the drought and plague. The people call her goddess, and they believe that she will heal them. She touches all that she can but is herself eventually overcome with the plague. The people then turn on her and begin to whisper that she is the accursed, having made herself into a goddess. This leads the priest to arrive at the palace, demanding an audience with the king who fears the priest's political power as a rival to his own. The priest announces that the horrible plight of Glome (enemies threatening, plague, drought, famine, and even lions roaming about) is due to the presence of evil in the land, a person having done something against the gods, the Accursed.

The king, of course, is convinced that the Priest intends to target him as the responsible party, so he becomes greatly relieved when the lots show that not the king but someone else in the king's household is the Accursed. Orual panics as it becomes clear that it is none other than Psyche. The Fox steps in and engages the Priest using his philosophical skills, showing the contradictions in what the Priest says about the Accursed: how the Accursed can be evil, yet also a pure sacrifice for the god of the mountain. But the Priest mocks the Fox for his cowardice in battle and undermines the force of his argument. Eventually, the king yields to the Priest's demand and permits Psyche to be taken for a sacrifice to the god of the mountain.

Orual is beside herself with grief, but she cannot undo the sentence. She visits her sister in her jail cell, and we begin to see the first glimpse not only of Orual's central vices, but also of her sister's extraordinary character, for Psyche, it seems, has had a deep conversation with the priest, and she shocks Orual by telling her that not all that the priest says is so crazy. Maybe the Fox does not know all. She goes on to explain that all her life she has felt the calling of the mountain, fantasizing about her golden castle as she is taken away to be a bride. She feels the call of the beautiful. And what if she is to be the god's bride?

Orual is shattered by all this talk of weddings on the night her sister is to be taken from her and left to die of starvation or to be torn apart by wild beasts. But she seems most concerned with the fact of Psyche's apparent composure. Why isn't Psyche wailing and holding onto Orual for dear life, as a mother would expect her child to do in such circumstances? Orual becomes bitter that Psyche does not attend to *her*.

Stepping out of the story, I want you to think about the extraordinary intellectual activity Pscyhe is carrying out under these shocking circumstances. She is merging in her mind the elements of the philosophy of the Fox, the religion of Ungit, and her own experience of her longing for the mountain, in effect creating a new syncretic understanding of how it all comes together, and, crucially, what it's all *for*.

For our next chapter, pay close attention to what occurs between Psyche and Orual on the mountain, and then on the discussions Orual has with Bardia and the Fox about what is to be done. Finally, notice the challenge that Orual makes to Psyche and what happens as a result.

CHAPTER TWENTY-FIVE

THE SISTERS' DUEL

(C. S. Lewis, *Till We Have Faces*, Pages 77-176)

We left off in our last chapter with Psyche being taken away as the Accursed to be sacrificed to the god of the mountain, the Shadowbrute. In a page straight out of Plato's *Phaedo*, Psyche has the most extraordinary discussion about the significance of death prior to her sacrifice. Orual succumbs to fainting and then fever, and only recovers days after Psyche has been left up on the mountain. Overcome with grief and a determination like Antigone's to make a proper burial of her sister, she persuades Bardia to join her on a trip up to the mountain and the holy tree.

On the way up the mountain something unusual happens to Orual. In spite of being grief-stricken and angry over her sister's death, as she approaches the mountain her heart is filled with joy, as though the air is on fire with it. She feels within herself the question, "And why should your heart not dance?" Orual feels that even she is beautiful, and that delight ought to be the response to the good of the world around her. But she comments to us, her readers, that this is just what the gods do to us—blow us up large before they prick and pop us.

Bardia is convinced it's all gods' business and no business of theirs, and Orual shoves the delight aside, intent on performing the rite for her sister's body. But as they approach the site, they find the chain, still closed, but no Psyche, not even torn clothes or bones. Nothing at all. Orual finds a path into the valley and follows it down to the river, where to her complete shock she finds Psyche standing on the other side.

Now, in thinking about the main argument of the book, one of the things Orual has to do is convince us that the gods expected her to be able to figure out what had happened to Psyche with insufficient evidence, and as such, their judgment against her is unjust. So, carefully review this section of the novel, the meeting of Orual and Psyche, and ask yourself whether there was evidence available to Orual that made Psyche's tale of her rescue by the god and life in the castle reasonable or not. For example, notice Psyche's physical and mental condition.

As their conversation proceeds, it becomes clear that Orual is unable to see the castle at all, and this raises a mutual suspicion between the two sisters. Psyche finally concludes that it is as her husband, the god, had said, while Orual wonders if Psyche isn't mad. Throughout the text, notice how Orual not only complains that she cannot tell if Psyche is mad or not, but that she seems irritated with Psyche for thinking of herself as a loyal wife to some god who won't reveal his face in the darkness. Orual's main concern seems to be to get Psyche away from the mountain, back with her. But she has failed to think about what they would do back in Glome (since as the Accursed, the people would presumably resend her back up the mountain), or whether Psyche's tale is in fact *true*, for if true, why would a sister demand that her recently married sister leave her husband and return home?

You'll note that from time to time Orual actually considers whether Psyche might not be telling the truth, but she seems irked that she is not able to see what Psyche can see. She's the motherly figure, after all. And then when Psyche says that she'll ask the god for Orual to be able to see, it becomes clear that Orual doesn't really *want* to see (pg. 123). In fact, she finds herself wondering which would be worse, to be mad or to be taken by that dark thing in the night. Finally, Orual orders Psyche to return to Glome with her, and Psyche firmly refuses, announcing that she now belongs to another and no longer takes orders from Orual. Notice the role reversal here and throughout this part of the text, as Psyche emerges more and more queen-like.

That night as Orual sleeps on the far side of the river, she awakens and heads to the river for a drink. And there she sees the castle, unlike any castle she'd ever heard about or seen (so it couldn't have arisen from her imagination). She realizes that Psyche is right, and wonders what the god will do to her for her doubt and hatred of him. But then the castle fades into the swirling mist, and she begins to wonder if she'd really seen a castle or not. After all, she'd barely awaken, and wouldn't it be just like gods to offer you a half-glimpse only to confuse you. Moreover, how does one riddle answer another riddle?

The next day she asks Bardia his opinion of the whole affair, though she is careful not to say a word about her vision of the castle the night before. Bardia feels that Psyche appears healthy and in her right mind, but that since the brute won't show his face, it's most likely that some monster has Psyche in its grasp and uses her at night. But she's happy, so what's the difference? Orual flies into one of her rages, for they are of divine blood, and no parents could endure their child becoming a whore, or, worse, the plaything of a monster. What does her happiness have to do with it?

Once they return to Glome, she consults the Fox on the matter, again careful not to reveal the part of the story where she saw the castle. Fox suggests that Psyche is mad, for it's ridiculous to believe that some god or shadowbrute has her in an invisible castle. When Orual asks whether some invisible things might not exist, the Fox answers her in philosophical categories: justice, love, friendship, virtue. But not castles. So, he suggests that the only reasonable answer is that Psyche is held by some ruffian up on the mountain, and she's either drugged or too demented to realize what's really happened to her. So, her subconscious mind has taken the old amber house fantasy and fashioned a delusion for her to make sense of her condition.

That evening Orual prays to the gods all night if only they will help her figure out what to do, what is real. But, as usual, there is only silence in the darkness. And so she concludes she'll have to figure it out herself. Now, it's worth asking whether this is an entirely fair conclusion, especially if the gods have already provided her with ample evidence of Psyche's true condition. This is where the evidential issue is crucial.

Orual mulls over the dilemma and realizes that she has incompatible versions of what's happening to Psyche from the Fox and from Bardia. Both stories cannot be right. Bardia thinks she's been taken by the shadowbrute, while the Fox thinks she's the plaything of a vagabond kidnapper. But they agree that nothing good comes to her at night . . . why else would it require that she not look at its face? (Could there be another reason?)

In spite of her knowledge that Psyche's joy is real, she concludes that it's her responsibility as a parent to decide for her child, and so she resolves to return to the mountain and force Psyche to come home, on pain of death if necessary. She is surprised and relieved when events occur to enable her to escape undetected yet again, so that she can return to the mountain.

When she sees Psyche again, Psyche reminds her of her prophecy that her god would do something to enable Orual to return. But Orual barely hesitates, focusing solely on what is to be done, no time for pondering new evidence. She urges Psyche to abandon her situation with the god, trusting to Orual's judgment. Psyche replies that she needn't pit herself against her husband, because they can all be together. Orual finally makes her move and announces to Psyche that it's a strange god who "dares not show his face." At this, Psyche becomes angry and defensive of her husband, "Dares not?" But Orual presses the question of why he won't show his face, and the reasonableness of a test to check on just who he really is. Orual offers Psyche the opinion of the Fox. Though moved, Psyche nevertheless insists that she is a wife now, and she knows her husband intimately, even if she's not seen his face. As such, she knows he's not a monster. Orual responds very negatively to Psyche's appeal to her own sexual knowledge, as though Psyche is ranking herself above Orual because Orual is an ugly virgin.

Orual continues her argument, insisting that Psyche lacks the courage to prove that her husband is really a god. Psyche admits that she does not know the reason for his hiding his face from her, but because he is good, she is sure that there is a reason currently unknown to her, his simple Psyche. She thinks she ought to trust him. Left with no remaining recourse to reason, Orual stabs herself in the arm, and threatens to kill both Psyche and herself unless Psyche returns with her.

Now, this appeal to force instead of reason is highly instructive. Ask yourself what this means for Orual's case. And notice, too, how differently Psyche acts now. She and Orual are on completely different planes morally. Again, we see how Psyche is so much more "queen-like." In order to save Orual's life, she finally relents, convinced that it's more likely that the god will forgive her than that she will succeed in restraining Orual.

The result you know well: the valley tears apart under the force of the god's wrath, the river swells to a torrent permanently dividing Psyche and Orual, and Psyche is cast out of paradise to wander the earth. And the god appears to Orual, so stunningly beautiful that Orual cannot bear to look. The god makes her feel that she always knew it was a god, that all her doubts were merely drummed up. And then he judges her: "You will know what you have done.

You too shall be Psyche." What do you think this means? Mull that over, as well as whether you think Orual is right to be angry at the god. Furthermore, what do you make of Psyche's confidence that her husband would forgive her? Was she right?

CHAPTER TWENTY-SIX

UNRAVELING A QUEEN

(C. S. Lewis, *Till We Have Faces*, Pages 177-294)

We left Orual in our last chapter having just persuaded Psyche to shatter her own happiness by disobeying the divine command. Psyche was cast out and condemned to wander the earth outside the god's protection, and Orual was left with the haunting judgment that she would know what she had done, because she too would be Psyche.

Unable to understand the judgment, Orual returns to Glome and tries to burn all her past with Psyche since the Great Offering. She restores Psyche's room to the way it was before all this happened. She furthermore takes up swordsmanship with Bardia, learning that the physical arts are much more useful for taming the conscience than philosophy. She determines to drive all the woman out of herself, to take on manly virtue, and, thus, to steel herself against the judgment weighing on her soul.

Suddenly, the king dies, the old priest dies, and she is Queen! She seals her monarchy with the battle that she manages to win, and decides to hide her face behind a veil. The mystery only deepens her grip on power and her resolve to destroy Orual and become the Queen. This inner self-destruction is worth a pause. What do you think accounts for it?

But she cannot wholly exclude the past from intruding into her new life, for she hears Psyche's cries at night, and then something truly extraordinary happens on her journey to Phars as she passes into Essur. She finds a temple to Istra, and the priest tells her a tale of a conspiracy between two sisters to deliberately destroy the happiness of Istra. And why did they do this? Because of their jealousy and spite. And in the story, they clearly saw the palace.

Orual is livid, now that her story has become "corrupted" as myth, and she determines to write the truth down. Thus is born Part I of our story. On pages 249-250 she concludes her book and summarizes her case against the gods. Let's review her argument.

Orual believes that the one thing in the world that she truly loved, Psyche, had been stolen from her by the gods. And then, rather than giving her a clear understanding of what Psyche's condition was, they forced her to guess. And because she guessed wrong, she was condemned. Add to that, the gods then put out a false story about what had actually occurred, making it appear that Orual was consumed with jealousy.

Orual concludes with a dilemma: the gods ought either to go away and leave us alone, or else they should show themselves openly and tell us clearly what they have in mind. Instead, they hover in dreams and mysteries and oracles. Why, she asks, "must holy places be dark places?" Now, this is an intriguing challenge—not just in pagan religion but for religion in general. Why is it that there's always mystery, sacrament, symbolism, and obscurity? It's not like Christianity fixes all of this with the mysteries of Baptism and Eucharist, as well as obscure texts like St. John's Revelation. What's the point of all this mystery? And do the gods, or God, just expect way too much of mere mortals like ourselves? How are we supposed to know what is expected of us? And what is it all for, anyway? Does Orual possibly have a point here?

We now embark on Part II of the book, and right away, we hear a different voice in Orual. For the first time in her life, she admits to wrongs, asserting that she had to add to the book or else she should leave this world perjured! Her memory had been awakened by the writing of the book, and the truth about the past coupled with her current efforts for moral reform bring about the beginning of the beginning for her, preparation for the divine surgery that is about to unfold. And it all begins with Redival.

Tarin, the boy many years before emasculated by the King for his love of Redival, turns up as the steward of a great kingdom, and he tells Orual of Redival's pain. Orual had written off her eldest sister on the grounds that she "had her curls." Orual's initial view of the world was cast in terms of her own ugliness, so what did Redival have to complain about? But in loving Redival, Tarin came to know that she felt left out of the inner circle of the Fox, Psyche, and Orual. Orual did nothing to include her, and when the King forced them to keep watch on Redival, she resented it. Orual is not stupid, of course; it's not like she thinks Redival was not responsible for her own choices. But Orual now considers human beings constitutionally, evaluating the role she played in forming Redival's character. And she knows now that she did her wrong.

Next we come to Bardia. After a lifetime of service to the Queen, he finally succumbs to death. Orual pays a call to Ansit, Bardia's wife, during her time of grieving. Lady Ansit blames the Queen for sucking the life out of Bardia, keeping him at the Pillar Room for late hours just to have him in her company. Orual is shocked to think that Ansit is jealous, and lifting her veil, thinks to quiet Ansit's insolence by showing her that she could have nothing for which to be jealous. But Ansit isn't that shallow a person, and she immediately reads in Orual's pained look the stunning fact that the Queen also loved Bardia. For a moment they embrace, joined in their mutual loss. But not for long, as the

FAITH & REFLECTION

sword thrusts of blame return. Orual thinks to halt the inquisition by counter-accusing Ansit of never having said anything about it, of Bardia never asking to be relieved early. Orual claims she would have released him, had she only known of the hardship he bore for her.

Ansit gazes at the Queen in surprise, and asks how she could be so wise a queen and know nothing of true love, for Ansit to love her husband is to love her husband according to who he is, not what she would make him. He was the Captain of the Queen's Guard. To take him away from that would be to take him away from himself, and that's not love at all. Ansit has the sudden insight that perhaps that sort of love—the devouring kind—is what gods and royals know, but it is not the love of the common people.

Orual reflects on what she's heard from Ansit. Her love for Bardia, she painfully realizes, was nine-tenths hatred. Why? Because she knew that Bardia longed to be home, that Bardia somewhat shallowly loved his wife for her beauty, and in her jealousy, she used this against him for subtle mockery. She was indeed the devourer. Like Ungit herself, using up the Ungit girls until they were wasted away, so the faceless Queen used up her subjects. She is Ungit.

She dreams of the Pillar Room and her father, a dream of her digging into deeper and still deeper Pillar Rooms, each one smaller and earthier than the next, digging down into the origins of Ungit, the goddess who emerged from the earth. The layers of Orual's defenses are removed one by one, until finally they come to a tiny Pillar Room with the mirror. When she beholds herself, she sees Ungit. She is the shadowbrute, the devourer, sucking the vitality out of the people and giving nothing in return.

Overcome with guilt and shock, she drags her ragged form to the river Shennit, planning to drown herself and put everyone out of her miserable grasp. But no sooner does she approach the river than she hears the voice of the god again. She must not do it, but must instead die before she dies, for after death there is no escaping Ungit. Ungit is there also.

Now, let's step back from the story and think about Ungit. What does Ungit *mean*? This is the question. How is Ungit present in death as well as in life? Mull that over carefully. Remember that Ungit enabled the peasant woman to find remission from guilt through the sacrificial bird's blood being poured over her. But why can't Orual find comfort?

Orual concludes that she needs to die before she dies in the sense that she must put to death her vices, which she admits are many. Following the path of Socratic philosophy (notice, not Stoic), she pursues a program to rid herself of vices and replace them with virtues. But try as she might, she doesn't get very far into her day, when her vices return with a vengeance. She cannot improve herself. Why do you think that is? What's wrong with her? On pages 282-283 Orual wonders if just as people are made ugly in body maybe they are also made ugly in soul, so blessed are the ones who are born good.

But I wonder if she ought not perhaps to remember what the god told her the first time, that she would know what she had done, that she too would be Psyche. Has Orual come to grips with what she did to Psyche? Can she really rid herself of vice, when she hasn't admitted the most fundamental vice in her life? Doesn't she have to die to her old self in order to establish a new one? Maybe she lacks the understanding to fully grasp how far down her vice really goes, that the love she considered the purest was in fact the most vile.

It's not long after this that Orual experiences her labor vision dreams in which she undergoes hugely difficult labors (the seed sorting, and the golden fur of the rams), but someone else seems to appear in the background benefiting from them. And then comes the most significant vision, which she is sure is no dream. She simply walks into the burning sands and crosses the long desert with her bowl to travel to the deadlands and retrieve the holy water which she is then to bring back to the living lands to make Ungit beautiful. In this task, Orual feels that she can perhaps finally make things right with Ungit.

But as she approaches the great mountain, the bird circles above her and asks what she carries. To her surprise she finds that the bowl is now her book, her complaint against the gods. The bird tells her to follow him, for now indeed her complaint will be heard. She is finally to have her day in court to make her case against the gods!

She is brought into a vast dark chamber, but in the forefront she can see the shades of Batta, the King, and the Fox. She is placed on a high dais and stripped of all clothing, for before the gods all secrets are revealed. She raises her book and realizes that it's not the book she wrote at all, but some withered tiny thing. But she cannot help but read it, and as she reads, she realizes that the words coming from her lips are the truth.

What truth does Orual reveal to the court and to herself? Answer: that her deepest vice was her jealousy of the gods for taking Psyche for themselves. Orual seems to have thought that Psyche's divine beauty belonged to her, and she exclaims that it would be better that the gods in fact drank the blood of our loved ones (the way the myths stated things happened) rather than took them from us. Moreover, she admits full well that no signs could have made a difference to her, because she didn't want to know the truth. She wanted Psyche for herself, end of story. Psyche's happiness was not relevant to Orual, for what could Psyche's happiness mean to Orual unless Orual controlled it? Psyche was the property of Orual, and it was divine theft for the gods to steal her away.

After she's read and reread the book, working herself into hysteria, the presiding god declares it is enough, and asks her if she has her answer. And she admits that yes, she does. What is the answer that Orual comes to? How is it that the gods do not have to give her any other answer than the reading of her own book?

Chapter four of Part II of *Till We Have Faces* fully explicates the answer to this question, so let's just take a quick peek before concluding today's chapter. On page 294, Orual explains that her complaint was itself the answer. For the first time in her life Orual had told the truth, but it brought no joy—only pain. And then she answers the question that drove her from the beginning of the book: why do the gods not speak openly to us, nor let us answer?

Her answer: "Till that word can be dug out of us, why should they hear the babble that we think we mean? How can they meet us face to face till we have faces?" Let's begin with the end or purpose that the gods have for us, the question we've been asking from the beginning of this book: *what is religion for?* What, in other words, is the meaning of it all? Orual reveals that the gods wish to know us face to face, as persons. But to know us as persons, we have to first *be* persons. And to be a person is to be an agent capable of love. But how can we love, when we twist love into devouring? And how can we cease devouring if we cannot see the truth of ourselves. If we lack a face, how can the gods speak with us face to face? How can they speak plainly when we will not hear it?

Just imagine if some god had come to Orual in her earlier days, just dressed like an ordinary person, and told her what her true vices were and how she had crushed Psyche. What would she have done? Well, we know what she thought of the priest of Aphrodite. We know further that when Ansit told her the truth, she thought of impaling her. Until we're *ready* for the truth, willing to admit it, it doesn't do any good for us to hear it.

We're a lot like Orual, aren't we? How much do we use the people we claim we love only to devour their strength and life? How often do we use our positions of power to crush those for whom our power was given? Are we any better than Orual with all of our justifications and self-deceptions? Is Lewis perhaps painting a rather true picture of the way we really are? Are you Ungit?

CHAPTER TWENTY-SEVEN

THE FACE OF THE GOD

(C. S. Lewis, *Till We Have Faces*, Pages 253-309)

Before reading this chapter, it's probably worth rereading all of Part II of *Till We Have Faces*, so that you can pull together the full set of themes and the sequence leading up to Orual's remarkable admissions that culminate in her realization why the gods hide themselves from us. Until the nugget of truth can be dug out of us, how can we approach the gods? If we will not speak the truth to ourselves, how can we tell it to them? We cannot approach the god, the purest and highest Person, until we have the face of a real person.

Orual realizes that she, like we, is Ungit, faceless. The religion of Ungit has a powerful effect when used properly—it reveals one's sin. If you are familiar with the way St. Paul interprets the effect of the Jewish Law, it's quite similar. In his Roman letter, he says, "By the Law comes the knowledge of sin." Orual is now ready, ready to face the truth not now as idea, but as person, first in the person of the one she hurt the most, Psyche, and then before the god.

But we begin not with the god nor with Psyche, but with the Fox! And we see the Fox's confession to Orual, which should be instructive. How shall philosophy fare against the god's judgment? Fox admits to Orual on page 295 his own failing as her teacher. He had always said that the myths were just lies of poets, that Ungit's a false image. But now he knows that she is a true image of the Ungit within. But that says nothing about the real gods. And then he makes the truly stunning admission: he claimed knowledge when he knew nothing. He didn't know why the religion of Ungit had the effects it had on the people of Glome—how they found redemption and comfort in her. But he never admitted he didn't know; he acted like he knew it was all a lie. Yet all the time, for all its dark mystery, the religion of Ungit was closer to the truth than his "trim" sentences, for the priest knew that there had to be sacrifices, that the approach to the gods was most costly, because they will have a man's heart. But that costs everything, and only the blood religions show this. The Fox admits that he was glib.

We've talked in this book before about the similarities and differences between religion and philosophy, and you might have noticed how both philosophy and religion demand truth in the inner man. But here is a definite difference, for religion addresses the question of our approach to the gods, whereas the best philosophy seems to do is address their existence, their nature, our existence, our nature, and the fact of the vast difference. It's worth asking why that is, why philosophy with its emphasis on ideas never seems quite to get all the way to the personhood of the gods. Philosophy can tell you what love is, but can it teach you to love? Philosophy can tell you what the gods are, but can it help you to love them?

Fox feels now as though he fed the girls on words, but words refer to real things, and, strangely enough, the imagery of the priest was far closer to the real things than his words. His reflections on the "divine nature" never quite approached divine personhood, did they?

FAITH & REFLECTION

Fox asks Orual for her forgiveness, and Orual—so soon full of the realization of her own devouring darkness—casts his request to the side and begs his forgiveness for what she did to him, devouring the life from him and never permitting his return to his daughter and homeland. Fox easily forgives her and then says to her that it is time to take her before her judges. She made her case against the gods, and now it is their turn to make their case against her.

Orual no longer has any misperceptions about what she deserves, but she makes a small mistake when she says, "I cannot hope for mercy." The Fox rebuffs her, for were the gods to give us our true desert—real justice—we should be completely undone. Somehow, hope remains.

Fox takes her into the antechamber to await the judgment. He shows her the paintings on the wall, which have a strange connection to the dream visions she'd been having prior to the court hearing. As she gazes at the pictures, she realizes that they are moving—almost alive—only the central character in each picture is not Orual, but Psyche. First, she sees her attempted suicide in the river, only this time it is Psyche at the shore. Orual shouts out not to do it (just what the god told her, remember), and Psyche relents. Second, she sees Psyche imprisoned sorting out the seeds, only without the agony that Orual had experienced. As she looks closer, she realizes that ants are helping her sort. In the third, she sees Psyche creeping along trying to acquire the golden fur of the rams, when, suddenly, they sense an intruder and head off in the other direction, leaving their fur on the briars for Psyche. And finally, she sees the desert, but the figure of Orual is but a shadow, Psyche the real person. Psyche carries the bowl and Orual her book. The eagle was waiting for Psyche and brought to her the water of death.

The Fox asks Orual if she understands the meaning of the pictures, and Orual grasps that while Psyche struggled with the tasks that the gods had given to her, another (Orual herself) bore all the anguish. Recall that the god had told Orual that she, too, would be Psyche. Now, pay very close attention to Orual's reaction to this on page 301. Instead of storming around in a fury of jealousy and spite at the unfairness of it all, we see a wholly new Orual who gives thanks that she has been permitted to carry this burden for Psyche. Fox asks her if she'd rather have had justice, since she toiled and Psyche reaped the reward. Orual now understands that justice pales before the power of love.

They look up on the final wall, and there they see Psyche finishing the last task given to her, that she must go down into the deadlands without saying a word to any other person and retrieve beauty in a casket from the Queen of Death to bring back to the surface for Ungit to make her beautiful. They watch as Psyche faces her own demons, her own vices. You didn't think that Psyche was perfect, did you? No, Psyche too has flaws, which emerged over and over again in her life until she finally violated the command of her husband. We can decipher her flaws and how she has now overcome them by noting what three past temptations are placed before her again on her path into the deadlands.

First, the people: "Istra, goddess, heal us, be an oracle to us!" Second, the Fox: "Psyche, don't listen to all this mythic babble. Follow me up out of this false land and back to reality." Third, Orual: "Oh Psyche, my child, come back to your mother, to the world in which we were happy, come back to Maia." What is in common to these three temptations? In each case, how did Psyche respond in the past versus the silence she responds with now? You see, Psyche was too impressionable, too easily moved by others, ultimately shown in her listening to Orual. One wonders why Psyche didn't just tell her husband of Orual's plan and together they decide what to do about it!

But now Psyche resists each impulse, reliving the pain of her past choices. Watching all this in horror, Orual realizes just how much damage they did to the poor girl, how their jealousy that the gods should want Psyche for themselves drove them (the people, the Fox, and Orual) to such inanity. For the gods are beautiful, and the more their beauty is shown, the more mortals will be drawn to them. And in the drawing will arise friends, parents, spouses, and children all raising one voice to thwart their communion with the gods.

Having completed the final task, Psyche returns from the deadlands to approach Orual. Again, the transformation in Orual is evident in that she falls on her face before her sister, recognizing that Psyche is indeed now a goddess. Orual immediately admits her crime against her, for she had tried to make her into a mere thing, a possession. Orual confesses, "I never wished you well, never had one selfless thought of you. I was a craver."

But Psyche lifts Orual to her feet explaining that she has not yet given to her the casket that will make Ungit beautiful. Psyche hands Orual the casket, and when she touches Psyche's hands, she feels the same divine sensations that Psyche had felt when she'd first encountered the god and his invisible people in the valley. Orual feels that Psyche is both herself and more than herself, and then realizes that she is all the Psyches she'd ever been (and then some) all completed as one whole Psyche. (You might remember a version of this theme from *A Severe Mercy* in the discussion of the whole Davy in death.) But Orual also realizes she's a goddess, or perhaps better, a *real woman*, for the completion of womanhood is to step up to the final altar in presentation to the One for whom we were created. And we are all feminine to him.

Orual notices a change in the palace. All the glory and radiance she saw in Psyche is eclipsed as the entire hall flushes with the approach of the god. Orual is pierced through with the fulfillment of what she'd first rejected up on the mountain: terror, joy, overpowering sweetness. She feels completely unmade and then realizes that not even Psyche counts now. And yet, Orual thinks, Psyche does so count, but not for her own sake, but for the sake of the god who approaches the hall.

Orual describes the god as both dreadful and beautiful, nay, even stronger, that the god is dread and beauty itself. Remember, desire is made for the sake of something, for the beautiful. Are we to believe that beauty is not itself something? Not someone, when all our most beautiful loveliness is found in the face of our own beloved? Should not those beauties point to that ultimate beauty who is Beauty Himself, the god?

Orual realizes, finally, for whom she was made. All that was—and all that would be—had been made by him and made for his sake. Their ultimate joy could therefore only be found in community with the god. The gods don't steal people away, as she had erroneously charged, for we were made for them in the first place. Can a woman spite her own femininity in that she is made for the man? Can a man spite his own masculinity in that he is made for the woman? And can Man spite his own nature, when he is made for the god?

Orual looks into the pool before her and sees two pairs of feet and two faces, but they are both Psyche, one clothed, the other naked, but both so beautiful. And then the god speaks, "You also are Psyche." Her redemption was complete, for as she confessed the ugliness of her soul, her identity with Ungit, the beauty from the deadlands that Psyche brought for her, had, through death to her Ungit-self, transformed Orual into a complete woman, beautiful without as she was now beautiful within. The god had judged Orual, but not with justice, for justice yearns for a wholeness that it cannot supply. Only love can fill the emptiness of a person and transform that person into joy.

Orual finds herself back in Glome, and she scrawls a few last words in the second part of her book. We will examine them and complete this final chapter. She tells us that she ended the first book with the words, "no answer." But now she understands why the god utters no answer: he is himself the answer. What good are words, when the one for whom the words were forged is present? What can be lacking before his face? In his loveliness all questions die away, because he is himself the answer to them all.

BIBLIOGRAPHY

(WORKS CITED IN ORDER OF FIRST TEXTUAL APPEARANCE)

John Stuart Mill. *On Liberty*. Simon & Brown, 2012.

Plato. *Apology* (The Last Days of Socrates). Penguin, 2011.

Plato. *Phaedo*. Penguin Classics, 1993.

St. Thomas Aquinas. *Summa Contra Gentiles*. Notre Dame, 1991.

St. Ignatius. *Letter to the Smyrnaeans*.
    http://www.newadvent.org/fathers/0109.htm.

Aristotle. *Nicomachean Ethics*. Tran. By Roger Crisp. Cambridge University
    Press, 2000.

St. Augustine. *Confessions*. New City Press, 2001.

Constitution of the United States of America

John Locke. *Essay Concerning Human Understanding*. Oxford, 1979.

John Locke. *Discourse of Miracles*. Stanford, 1958.

David Hume. *Enquiry Concerning Human Understanding*. Cambridge, 2007.

C. S. Lewis. *Miracles*. HarperOne, 2009.

David Hume. *Dialogues Concerning Natural Religion*. Hackett, 1998.

Aristotle. *Metaphysics*. Oxford, 1924.

Bertrand Russell & Copleston, "A Debate on the Argument from
    Contingency." http://www.ditext.com/russell/debate.html

C. S. Lewis. *The Problem of Pain*. HarperOne, 2001.

Peter Kreeft. *Angels (and Demons)*. Ignatius, 1995.

St. Thomas Aquinas. *Summa Theologica*.
    ww.newadvent.org/fathers/0126.htm.

Sheldon Vanauken. *A Severe Mercy*. Harper & Row, 1977.

St. Justin Martyr. *Apologia*. http://www.newadvent.org/fathers/0126.htm.

T. S. Eliot. "Choruses from the Rock." *Collected Poems*. Harcourt Brace
    Jovanovich, 1991.

Thomas Howard. *Christ the Tiger*. Ignatius, 2005.

C. S. Lewis. *Till We Have Faces*. Harcourt Brace & Company, 1980.

Epictetus. *Enchiridion*. Trans. By George Long. Prometheus Books, 1995.

René Descartes. *Meditations on First Philosophy*. Cambridge: 1996.

ABOUT THE AUTHOR

Jeffrey Tiel, Ph.D., is an associate professor of philosophy at Ashland University in Ashland, Ohio. He previously taught at the United States Military Academy in West Point, NY, as well as Vanderbilt University in Nashville, TN. He is an award-winning teacher, known for bringing ancient ideas to life. He is the author of *Philosophy of Human Nature*, as well as the supernatural thriller, *The Search for Melchizedek*.

Made in the USA
Lexington, KY
14 September 2019